Contents

Preface *by Michael Marland*　　　　　　　　　　vii

1 INTRODUCTION　　　　　　　　　　　　　　1
What is ICT?　　　　　　　　　　　　　　　　1
What is this book about?　　　　　　　　　　　1
Why could this book be useful?　　　　　　　　2
Our school setting　　　　　　　　　　　　　2
Our whole school objectives　　　　　　　　　4
The school learning culture and ICT　　　　　　4
Learning across the school　　　　　　　　　　6
Areas of strength in ICT at Hampstead School
　identified by OFSTED March 2000　　　　　　8

2 LEADERSHIP　　　　　　　　　　　　　　10
Why is leadership crucial to the development
　of ICT in schools?　　　　　　　　　　　　10
Governors' support is crucial　　　　　　　　13
How can I give a lead?　　　　　　　　　　　14
ICT across the curriculum　　　　　　　　　　20

3 MANAGEMENT　　　　　　　　　　　　　22
Why use ICT for management in school?　　　　22
What are the challenges of using ICT?　　　　24
Case study 1 – How we store data safely at
　Hampstead School　　　　　　　　　　　　26
How can ICT assist us in the production
　of documents and publications?　　　　　　28
How can we use ICT to analyse our examination
　results and use this to raise teachers' expectations
　and students' achievement?　　　　　　　　29
Case study 2 – ICT in examination administration
　at Hampstead School　　　　　　　　　　　29
How can we best use ICT for budgeting and finance?　31
Case study 3 – Using ICT for budgeting and finance　32

How can we best use ICT to assist us in
  curriculum modelling, planning and timetabling? 33
Case study 4 – ICT and the timetabler 33
How can we use ICT to assist us in improving
  attendance and punctuality? 35
Case study 5 – Using ICT to analyse
  attendance and punctuality 35
How can we use ICT to assist with cover
  for absent colleagues? 36
Case study 6 – Using ICT for cover 36
How can we use ICT for the School Improvement Plan? 37
Case study 7 – ICT for department development
  and improvement planning 37
How can we use ICT for assessment and target setting? 40
Case study 8 – The use of ICT for assessment 40
How can we use ICT for quality control:
  monitoring and evaluation? 43

4 ICT AS A TOOL FOR ACTIVE LEARNING   48
ICT as scaffolding 49
Case study 9 – Science 50
A process model of learning 53
Stages of the do–review–learn–apply cycle 54
Taking advantage of ICT 57
Case study 10 – Independent Learning Centre 57
Conclusion 58

5 LEARNING ENVIRONMENTS AND TYPES OF SOFTWARE   60
Generic and specific software 61
Learning environments 63
Case study 11 – Design Technology 63
From instruction, through construction to
  co-construction 65
Case study 12 – Science 66
Case study 13 – Maths 68
The balance of control 70
Conclusion 71

6 WHAT IS ICT CAPABILITY?   73
IT becomes ICT 73
Strands of capability 74
Case study 14 – Art 77
Progression in ICT 78

Managing ICT in the Secondary School

by
Tamsyn Imison and Phil Taylor

Publishing Ltd

JOHANNESBURG   BLANTYRE   GABORONE
IBADAN   PORTSMOUTH (NH) USA   CHICAGO

Heinemann is a registered trademark of Reed Educational & Professional
Publishing Ltd

Text © Tamsyn Imison and Phil Taylor, 2001
With contributions from Geoff Berridge, Judy Brophy, John Curruthers,
Mark Everett, Florence Fineberg, Anne Goode, Simon Hunt, Katharine Imison,
Noel Jenkins, Ben Kestner, Poppy Mayer, Mark Mayne, Sally Millward,
Ben Moore, Fabiola Pilli, Debbie Price, Carla Prince, Sally Shippham,
Mark Southworth and Margaret Tettey.

First published in 2001

05 04 03 02 01
10 9 8 7 6 5 4 3 2 1

British Library Cataloguing in Publication Data
A catalogue record for this book is available from the British Library

ISBN 0 435 80061 2

Typeset by Wyvern 21 Ltd, Bristol
Printed and bound by Biddles Ltd, Guildford

Acknowledgements
The publishers would like to thank the following for permission to reproduce
copyright material:
The British Educational Communications and Technology Agency (BECTA) for
the list on p. 90; the Office for Standards in Education (OFSTED) and Hampstead
School for excerpts from the Hampstead School inspection report on pp. 11, 12,
29, 31, 35 and 37 (A full copy of the report can be obtained from Hampstead
School, Westbere Road, London, NW2 3RT.); Dr Reg North for the list on p. 103
that first appeared in his book *Managing Information Technology: The Role of the IT
Coordinator* (1990), University of Ulster; the Secondary Heads Association for the
SHA IT policy on pp. 14–18.

The publishers have made every effort to contact copyright holders. However, if
any material has been incorrectly acknowledged, the publishers would be pleased
to correct this at the earliest opportunity.

Tel: 01865 888058 www.heinemann.co.uk

Case study 15 – Music 81
Conclusion 82

7 A CROSS-CURRICULAR APPROACH TO ICT 84
Curriculum models for ICT 84
The guiding principles of cross-curricular ICT 87
From interference to enhancement 88
The ICT programme at Hampstead School 89
Case study 16 – Modern Languages 92
Case study 17 – A student's development 96
Conclusion 97

8 MANAGING ICT ACROSS THE CURRICULUM 99
The ICT team 99
Case study 17 – History 100
Monitoring and evaluating ICT across the curriculum 102
Managing ICT resources 103
Case study 18 – ICT Network Manager and Support 105
ICT documentation 106
The funding of ICT 108
Conclusion 109

9 STAFF DEVELOPMENT IN ICT 111
Improvement and change 112
Case study 19 – Geography 113
Acquiring ICT skills 116
Case study 20 – Head of Year 116
ICT teamwork as staff development 118
Coping with the range of software 119
Case study 21 – English 121
Conclusion 122

10 THE 'SCHOOLS' OF THE FUTURE 124
The schools of the future must deliver for the future –
 they must deliver key skills, particularly ICT 124
Leaders at all levels need the qualities exhibited by all the
 best world leaders if they are to radically reform schools 126
So how should our 'schools' be organised? 128
Teachers need to be autonomous lead-learners
 confident enough to actively support the development
 of ICT and other key skills 129
The new curriculum will emphasise skills
 and will require far more participant assessment 130

Suggestions for a new curriculum   130
Key points   133
Main questions   134

APPENDICES   **135**
Appendix 1 – Hampstead School ICT Policy   135
Appendix 2 – Hampstead School ICT Codes   140
Appendix 3 – Hampstead School Cross-curricular   142
ICT Map (1999–2000)

References and Bibliography   **146**

Index   **149**

Preface

Secondary schools have rarely had to face such a deep, wide-ranging and rapid external development which makes such major demands on the curriculum as the world-wide complex growth of ICT. The place of ICT in the world today requires school-wide recognition through all aspects of school life: curriculum planning, staff deployment, school organisation, the specific teaching of ICT skills, and its support in most aspects of the whole-school curriculum. This is a major school management challenge. All schools have been addressing this, but almost all are now reviewing and re-planning their ICT policy.

Heinemann School Management is a systematic and wide-ranging series of books written to enable those working in all management positions in schools, including teaching and support staff. The series aims further to improve the in-school study of policies and practices and to enhance the quality of the overall work of the school by a methodical and relevant study of educational needs, relevant research, current practice, new developments, and successful ways of establishing those developments and managing them. The series is well recognised and widely used. It has been formally praised by the School of Education at Kingston University as having 'pioneered the academic study of School Management'.

This practical exploration and exposition of the uses of ICT across the whole secondary school is a major contribution to whole-school curriculum planning and staff management. In the past, external forces and curriculum-planning difficulties often sadly led to a fragmented secondary curriculum that was a collection of separate school 'subjects' lacking the desirable coherence. Developments such as the Bullock Report's 'Language Across the Curriculum' and the National Association for Pastoral Case's 'Pastoral Curriculum', or the central government's 'Citizenship' curriculum demonstrate the conceptual, planning and implementation difficulties of whole-school curriculum planning.

Imison and Taylor have faced these long-standing difficulties together with the current challenge of ICT and successfully show in their text how a school can truly plan *across* the curriculum. ICT is not added on as a separate 'subject', but as an integral key aspect to all courses within an over-arching curriculum and school management policy that values and uses ICT. The authors detail how the best development of ICT teaching is in the context of the school's subject courses, both strengthening the teaching of those subjects and at the same time realistically developing the pupils' ICT concepts, skills and usage. Thus, the book brings together 'learning through' and 'learning about' in a detailed and wholly realistic way, one which has practical and positive proposals for a school's ICT team working with each of the subject course departments and all of the staff. The authors also demonstrate the importance of a whole-school ICT policy as a means of valuing students, for study and thinking skills, for library-user education and for the school's work with the wider communities it serves, including adults, minority ethnic communities and primary schools. A fully developed ICT policy is crucial for this new century's multi-ethnic Britain.

The two main authors have demonstrated very successfully at Hampstead School in London that these ideas and ways of delivery really do work well. Dame Tamsyn Imison has long experience in secondary school leadership, has participated in the important ICT Policy Group which developed the ICT Policy for the Secondary Headteachers Association, and has just retired to become a consultant on Educational Strategy. Co-author Phil Taylor has for many years developed and led new technology and independent learning both in secondary schools and in Higher Education. They have woven contributions into this book from a significant number of teachers and administrators who have worked on aspects of ICT at Hampstead. This is a large comprehensive school with a range of challenges.

Thus, *Managing ICT in Secondary Schools* is truly a whole-school book for a whole-school approach. The overall concept, realistic understanding of school challenges and needs, and the detailed practicality demonstrate how secondary schools can ensure that ICT does not offer 'interference' to existing subject courses and overall learning programmes, but a real enhancement of them.

Michael Marland

1 Introduction

What is ICT?

Information and communications technology (ICT) is an increasingly powerful means to enhance our abilities to think, to learn, to communicate and to use our brains creatively and logically. ICT provides the means by which we can search out vast stores of up-to-date, relevant as well as archive information. It makes it easy for us to get in touch with world experts in every field. It gives every school the opportunity of becoming instantly recognised world-wide. Our experience at Hampstead School has included positive and constructive comments on science software from California, Hawaii and other parts of the world. Visitors have come to us from Argentina, China, Taiwan, Australia, Germany and Sweden as a result of seeing our website. The key German textbook for teaching English uses pages from our website.

What is this book about?

This is a case study of the ways one successful comprehensive school has developed and used expertise in ICT across the whole school to improve performance and raise achievement. It is also about enthusiasm, about innovation and the excitement of learning. What we are doing is not so amazing that others cannot do the same. Many may well be doing better. If that is so, we want to hear from you and learn from you. What we are doing is extremely replicable in other schools and different settings. It is useful to compare practice and we are still learning and improving. We hope that this book will encourage readers to contact us: http://www.hampsteadschool.org.uk or e-mail us at: enquiries@hampsteadschool.org.uk to tell us your best practice or suggestions. Sadly, in schools many of us continually reinvent the wheel.

As we are both associated with the Secondary Headteachers Association (SHA), and as Tamsyn Imison was Chair of the SHA ICT Committee from its inception until 1999, we have included the SHA Policy thinking within the chapter on leadership and acknowledge the significant contribution of all the members of that Committee. The SHA ICT Committee was set up to consider key issues and policy in this crucial area, by John Dunford as President of SHA, and the group produced a list of useful questions for schools to consider. These are also included in the Leadership chapter.

We have divided the book into ten chapters – this introduction; six chapters on leadership, management, ICT as a tool for active learning, learning environments and types of software, ICT capability, and a cross-curricular approach; a core chapter embracing the whole curriculum on developing ICT capability across the curriculum; a chapter on staff development and training; and a final chapter on the schools of the future.

Why could this book be useful?

We hope that by presenting a case study of ICT capability and its use at one moment in time we may give some practical ideas or encouragement to all those on the same journey as ourselves. We think there should be more case studies by practising teachers. The TTA has done a lot to encourage this approach and there is also the National Grid for Learning (www.ngfl.gov.uk), but it is always interesting to get a birds-eye view of another school's experience.

It is also interesting at a time in this new millennium, when schools are transforming their practice, to record where we are now. In a very short time this moment will be significant history recording a powerful transition. We will look back and think, 'is this where we began?'

Our school setting

Hampstead School is an inner city comprehensive in Cricklewood, London – an area beautifully described by Zadie Smith, a recent student of ours, in her best-selling novel *White Teeth*. The rich multi-ethnic and varied social mix arises from a complex population. There is a well-established traditional village group, some gentrification, small enclaves of minority communities who retain their own customs and practices as well as a challenging group from a newly extended adjacent social priority estate used by the borough as a ghetto (we are right up against the borough boundary). We also have a more varied mix of people who have relatively recently found refuge through the borough's supportive policy towards asylum seekers. We have 135 students in this category, nearly one third of these arriving as unaccompanied minors. 60% of our roll (just 20% in 1985) is made up of students from ethnic minorities, 18% of whom are at stages 1 & 2 of language acquisition. Students now speak over 78 different languages and dialects.

Our ratio of girls to boys is 54:46 – not as significant as in other local mixed schools but, recognising that there are 23 more forms of entry for girls than boys locally, this will always be a key issue. We have traditionally taken children from over 40 feeder primary schools. 33% of our intake is registered for free school meal entitlement. There are 63 students with a statement of special needs: 5% of our roll. Over 400 pupils are on the SEN register at stages 1 to 4, comprising 20% of our roll. Over 50% gain five or more A* to C at the end of Year 11. Well over 90% of our Year 11 students stay on post 16 (70% in our own inclusive Sixth Form, 25% in other Sixth Forms and local Colleges.) From our own Sixth Form of 250 we send about 80 students from academic courses on to Higher Education, including Oxbridge, each year. About 40 students are successful on a range of vocational courses and also progress on to Higher and Further Education and Training.

With such a rich mix of talents, culture and background as well as social challenge, we are always looking to enlarge our vision and capacity. We must provide better learning opportunities for all – students and staff – and develop that 'sparkle in the eye' and tangible excitement that is exhibited by Creative Practitioners, particularly those who embrace the new technologies, and transmits itself like the bees' dances to all in the 'learning hive'. In our last Short OFSTED Inspection (March 2000), the Inspectors found that 70% of all lessons observed were 'good' to 'very good'. (None of our current 70 minute lessons were seen long enough to be rated outstanding, although a significant number were assessed so by the Local Authority team who visited us in the Autumn of 1999.) The OFSTED banner headlines included:

'Enthusiastic and energetic teaching generates an enjoyment for learning.'

'Outstanding leadership and management set a challenge to which both staff and pupils rise.'

'Pupils use information communications technology very effectively as a tool to support their learning.'

The staff profile shows a majority of high attaining, strongly committed colleagues, with women and those from ethnic minorities well represented in senior positions. Staff expect to move on to further promotion or development. A significant number are currently studying, or have studied, for further degrees. They act as excellent role models for both staff and students. They all use ICT and consider themselves to be eager learners of ICT in their leadership, management, support and curriculum delivery roles.

 ## Our whole-school objectives

Our aims as a school are set out in the following 'statement of intent'. This is regularly revised by staff, governors, parents and students. The most significant thing about our aims is that we consider everyone to be part of the learning community.

Learning together achieving together

At Hampstead School everyone will strive to:
- enjoy the challenges and achievement of learning;
- develop individual strengths;
- experience academic, social and personal success;
- manage setbacks;
- develop consideration and co-operation within a stimulating and supportive environment and with the support of family and the wider community.

 ## The school learning culture and ICT

The OFSTED Inspectors told us in May 1996 and March 2000 that Hampstead School is a good and a very good school because of the quality of the teaching. We have achieved this because we are a 'learning' institution welcoming many ways of enhancing our teaching. ICT is a key to enhancing our teaching and it is delivered across the whole curriculum as an integral part of all courses and all teaching. If we are to develop teaching as an 'art' we have to be creative and innovative, and fully 'own' the teaching and learning process. We need to be very clear about expected outcomes. If all teachers are committed to continue their own learning, their teaching will improve, and this spreads across the whole institution, creating a powerful learning ethos. A key strategy for developing these teams of reflective learners is maximising the use of ICT for everyone. We are also extremely interested in the 'mirror effect' – the ways in which learners reflect back from lead-learners their excitement, enthusiasm and strategies for learning.

As we approach the 21st century we need new approaches to teaching and learning if we are to be successful in raising the achievement levels of all students, particularly those who find it hardest. We must enlist the active support of all partners in education – our students, their parents, governors, colleagues, support specialists, industry and community mentors, as well as student teachers, Higher Education partners and researchers. Many of these partners are excited and more experienced in using ICT than teachers. This is particularly true of most of our students who show no fear of learning new ways of doing things. A recent survey at our school showed that 70% have their own computers and 40% have Internet access. Our sixth formers studying AS and A2 level Electronics have regular links through both on-line and video conferencing with a tutor in Whitby. They manage this all themselves. Past results have been above national averages.

We must use a whole armament of strategies, especially new technologies and new partnerships, for managing learning. This requires us to establish true community learning centres where both adults and children learn together. The rigid boundaries existing around institutions, curricula, day and year structures will change. We are taking in our first wheelchair-bound student in September 2000 and the LEA is making a huge commitment to provide lifts and easy access for students and adults with physical disabilities. This will be a significant second step in providing access to the whole community as we already have both the technology and the expertise to train.

Action research can also be a reflective evaluation tool. This is certainly supported by Stenhouse, when he puts forward the case for research as the basis for teaching:

> 'Research gains accrue from the gradual accumulation of knowledge through the patient definition of error.'

> 'A decade of in-service education which neglects curriculum research will be wasting the greatest potential of an immense investment.'

> (Stenhouse, 1980, p. 244)

For us, writing this book together has been a piece of action research.

Vygotsky, Bruner and Glasersfeld's vision of learning as a true dialogue and interaction with others is very significant, particularly when we use ICT. The concept of the zone of proximal development – the region between what we know and what we want to know, and the idea of scaffolding and navigation, are made far clearer. As practitioners it clarifies our views and strategies for supporting timid learners, helps us understand our own learning, and sets an example to other colleagues.

Learning across the school

John Dewey in *Democracy and Education* says 'society not only exists by transmission and by communication, it exists *in* transmission and communication'. We are seeking to engage in learning that comes from talking and debating together in search of common understandings. In *How Children Think and Learn* (Wood, 1988, p. 225), the author comments on Piaget's legacy of 'the respect it inspires for children's capacities as learners and as architects of their own understanding' and their 'capacity for self correction and self instruction'.

Our experience is that, in using ICT across the school, we show we are valuing all students. It makes their courses fun. It gives lessons high status, especially when it involves others using the Web or video conferencing. Students and teachers become very proud of their work, increase their motivation and become actively involved in their own learning and progression. For the lowest attainers, if this leads on to another relevant, practically based course requiring independent learning using a variety of new technologies, they rapidly become confident learners.

We describe good learners as those confident enough or valued and supported enough to engage in real dialogues about learning. We are thinking of Vygotsky's view of co-operation with others and Bruner's view that 'the problem is not with competence but with performance', and that learning is amenable to improvement so we can be taught how to learn. This is critical, and teachers who are also learners are best equipped to support learning strategies. Learners are those who have been made to feel successful about learning. Teachers have to be learners to deliver ever newer, ever changing technologies, and often students are the lead learners!

We define teachers as supportive positive adult learners. They are prepared to understand and identify the needs of all students, and share with them the excitement of travelling from the known to the unknown. They prepare guides, maps and charts – far easier using a computer and new technologies, scaffolds and dictionaries to make sense for the student of the path they are following, the knowledge and skills they are accessing and the purpose of it all.

Hampstead School is a Technology College and a specialist school. It is perfectly obvious to anyone visiting a number of schools that each one is unique. Each school is determined by its particular context and ethos. The ethos comes from the vision, leadership and skills within each school. Schools in the UK retain significant flexibility despite a national curriculum, to organise the day structure, the groupings, the curriculum opportunities, the pedagogy and the inputs from parents, communities, business and industry as well as from Further and Higher Education. Schools take young people at different ages and send them on to the next stage at different times. Most importantly, schools select their own staff and have responsibility for staff development and staff opportunities.

Specialist schools began as Technology Colleges, but now exist in many forms – Language Colleges, Performing Arts and Sports Colleges. The magnet schools in the USA have not been an unqualified success, particularly when they have over-specialised and distorted the curriculum, or when they have become selective and deprived other schools of talented young people – the worst form of social engineering. Hampstead School applied to be a Technology College in 1995, wanting neither to have a distorted curriculum depriving young people of career choices nor to be selective, leaching talent from other local schools. There were three reasons why we applied.

Firstly, we have, as a school community, thought a lot about the future, about the impact of huge changes to the world of work and the need for dramatic changes to schools. We want to change the nature of our school now, not wait until change is imposed upon us. We believe that all schools will eventually become community learning centres where the majority of adults will have access. Over 50% of adults now are not in a full-time job. Very few jobs last more than six years. Most adults will need to continuously re-skill themselves in order to meet the increasing challenges for employability. The opportunities to change and develop both the site and buildings, technological resources and organisation of the school are limited but funding through the specialist schools programme can provide some of this. Our main focus from the £130,000 we raised ourselves and the money put in by the LEA on the instruction of the Government has been to develop the library into an exciting independent learning centre which also has the potential to support parents and our local communities. Everyone needs to become an independent learner. By focusing on ways of encouraging and developing active learning and independent study, we will provide young people, their parents and their communities with the skills and confidence to seize opportunities for both personal development and for employment.

Secondly, we are convinced of and have proved the huge value that new technologies can offer in motivating under-achievers, stimulating and challenging the often forgotten middle bands as well as the high fliers. There is support for boys, for girls, for ethnic minorities, for all students. We are using new technologies to deliver the whole curriculum. In our school, we have a broad and balanced core curriculum for years 7 to 11. The technological enrichment to all subjects has a far greater impact upon all children than a narrowing of focus to just a few. There are difficulties in fitting all subjects in, but we do ensure that all areas of experience are retained so that no child at the tender age of 13 has to make life choices which could restrict their future careers. We would prefer Key Stage 3 to be shorter and Key Stage 4 longer to give us greater flexibility. But the critical concern we have is to deliver quality teaching, using technologies so that all our students become active learners, comfortable with and in control of technologies in all subject areas so they can develop their own knowledge, understanding and abilities.

Thirdly, we are uncomfortable about receiving more than other schools and see this as a requirement on us to share facilities, knowledge and expertise with our link primary schools and neighbouring secondary schools as well as with other visitors whom we welcome. One example of this is our video conferencing link with a neighbouring primary school to support the Somali refugees and families of both schools. We are very pleased that in the second phase of Specialist School existence, a significant part of the funding available to us depends on new developments that are of value to others as well as ourselves.

We have had to make further bids at this second phase. Bidding has its benefits as well as its problems – making a school think through carefully what it wants to do, what resources it needs and what the success criteria should be – usually much broader than bald performance scores. Raising funding has also made us talk authoritatively with business and industry partners, improving mutual understandings and developing really valuable partnerships.

Other kinds of specialist colleges could also use their specialist input to infuse the whole curriculum. We hope our model will prevail!

Areas of strength in ICT at Hampstead School identified by OFSTED March 2000

A commitment from senior management to harness ICT as a tool for learning and for school improvement.
Evidence: Technology College status, investment in equipment and staff, lead person for ICT is a member of senior management.

A focus on using the acquisition of ICT skills in order to enhance learning within curriculum subjects.
Evidence: ICT skills taught entirely across the curriculum within subject contexts, ICT activities are subject-led.

Good basic ICT skills being developed by all students.
Evidence: KS3 assessments.

A team structure for co-ordinating ICT across the curriculum.
Evidence: Science, Maths, Design & Technology and Modern Languages departments each have their own ICT co-ordinator, and there is an additional cross-curricular ICT co-ordinator.

Staff who readily integrate ICT into their teaching and who wish to improve their ICT skills.
Evidence: ICT activities integrated into schemes of work, nearly 100% take-up for NoF ICT training.

An increasing range of subject-based expertise in the use of ICT.
Evidence: contribution to BECTA publication 'History Using IT', Delivery of Science INSET for Camden LEA.

A creative and developmental approach to ICT network management in order to provide good access for staff and students and exciting learning opportunities.
Evidence: over 1500 users registered on our networks, over 100 software titles, networked Internet access.

A desire to share facilities and expertise with others.
Evidence: hosting of several ICT events, ICT training for our main feeder primary school, provision of equipment and training for the Camden Somali Cultural Centre, ICT inset day for a local secondary school, PGCE students from the Institute of Education, BETT show presentations, book currently being written.

A commitment to the use of ICT to improve school administration and management.
Evidence: expanding administration networks, improving ICT facilities for staff, electronic registration system, monitoring of student progress.

A self-critical approach to evaluating what to do with ICT – there are many areas for improvement.
Evidence: challenging development plans for ICT.

2 Leadership

■■■ Why is leadership crucial to the development of ICT in schools?

Schools of tomorrow must prepare students to be effective world competitors. Our task is exciting and challenging. We have to do ten things:

1. Be fearless, take risks and innovate

2. Mobilise the intellectual, personal and social capabilities of all

3. Have a mission, a strategy for achieving it and ambitious goals and SMART targets by which we can monitor success

4. Develop learning communities

5. Build on the strengths of all staff and students by taking their learning seriously

6. Support staff and students' independent learning using peer counselling, work reviews, target setting and records of achievement

7. Use all available information and communication technologies

8. Develop independent learning centres and community resources maximising new technologies which support information retrieval, information manipulation and learning

9. Ensure that the core skills of literacy, numeracy and technology are sound

10. Ensure progression, credit accumulation and transfer

In the *Institute of Education Report* (Sammons et al, 1995), the authors have identified eleven key factors for effective schools. All of these depend upon good leadership. Five of these move the school towards becoming a learning institution:

1. Professional leadership from a leading professional which is firm and purposeful, with a participative approach

Michael Fullan, writing on *Leadership for Change* (1995), says:

> *'Effective principals extend as well as express what they value. They nurture a subtle process of enabling teachers to work together to generate solutions.'*

> *'The principal is working towards a learning organisation.'*

George Binney and Colin Williams in *Leaning into the Future* (1995) state:

> *'employees judge a manager's commitment to any change 10% on what he or she says and 90% on what he or she does.'*

They also talk about 'organisations developing the learning habit'. At Hampstead School, we have a powerful and large Senior Leadership Team. It is this team of eight which makes an impact:

> *'Outstanding leadership and management sets a challenge to which both staff and pupils rise.'* (OFSTED 2000, Hampstead School)

2. Shared vision and goals showing unity of purpose, consistency of practice, collegiality and collaboration

The whole staff are involved in establishing our constantly revised aim statement and joint policy development. Our Registered Inspector said, 'There is consistency of approach and policy across the whole school'. Our united view is that ICT must be a tool for all.

3. Concentration on teaching and learning

> *'Enthusiastic and energetic teaching generates an enjoyment for learning.'*
> (OFSTED 2000, Hampstead School)

All our teachers use ICT as an integral part of their teaching and our OFSTED inspectors were spoilt for choice!

4. Purposeful teaching which exhibits efficient organisation, clarity of purpose, structured lessons and adaptive practice

> *'A major reason for the success of the school is the high quality of much of the teaching. Pupils are keen to learn, make good progress and achieve standards that compare favourably with similar schools. The work seen in lessons reflects these standards...'*

Good examples of pupils using IT were observed in all year groups. Year 7 pupils learnt quickly how to use a spreadsheet in a mathematics lesson to help to plan the requirements and costs for a party. A very well-taught Year 8 geography lesson, as part of a well-planned sequence of lessons, developed the pupilsí use of a spreadsheet. An analysis of data on population growth in India was analysed and the results presented in a variety of graphical forms. Other Year 8 pupils were observed researching the history of the orchestra in a music lesson, using CD-ROMs and the Internet as sources of their information. Pupils have the opportunity to control by programming the movements of objects in design and technology. Good use was made of IT in a Year 9 art lesson, where the pupils experimented to show how different colours could affect mood. Pupils in a Year 9 French lesson were able to choose the software they would use to produce a leaflet about a club. Most were able to merge text and illustrations effectively. Skills in the use and application of IT develop well at Key Stage 4 from word-processing a curriculum vitae in a Year 10 careers lesson, using a spreadsheet to analyse the data obtained in a science experiment on electrical circuits, to exploring the effects of changes in environment in a Year 11 science lesson on inheritance and genetics. IT is also used regularly in the Sixth Form by students studying for GNVQ, and in many other subjects.'

(OFSTED 2000, Hampstead School)

A full copy of the OFSTED inspection report of Hampstead School can be obtained from Hampstead School, Westbere Road, London, NW2 3RT.

5. A learning organisation

This is the nub of it all. In a recent survey carried out by our Staff Development Task Group, 93% of staff said they wanted to continue with further studies and research. We have top sliced our funding for professional development, research and industry links funding which colleagues can bid for since 1996. Colleagues are encouraged to take further degrees. Since September 1996 we have been running our own in-house Masters Programme taught by colleagues from the International School Effectiveness Unit at the Institute of Education. ICT skills have been essential for participants to deliver quality assignments. It has also been a significant topic for in-house research by participants. With a staff eager to learn, the training and learning needed to be able to support students' learning becomes relatively easy. We have a sound personal development model of appraisal, which has been endorsed by our Investors in People status since 1999. We have encouraged the use of personal development folders by both staff and students.

Governors' support is crucial

We are extremely fortunate to have a Chair of Governors and a Governing Body who are strongly committed to ICT and to an integrated approach. Their influence is very important.

■ Statement from the Chair of Governors

I am an enthusiast for new technologies. My strong personal belief is that the use of these technologies has a profound impact on both teachers and those taught. I use ICT myself. The key differences this has made for me personally have been that:

- *I can communicate with a much wider group of people.*
- *In a work-related sense, I can use ICT to demonstrate my competence to others.*
- *In a more sociable sense, I can share and access information far more easily; for example, linking with other like-minded professionals or, accessing recreational organisations like proms on-line.*

I think ICT is a very important adjunct to teaching and a powerful tool for getting information. The presenting of consistent data in a visual, comprehensible form makes it possible for complex information to be accessible to all Governors including those with little prior knowledge. It allows Governors to analyse and interpret data easily, to look in detail at performance, and to use this, to work out the added value the school is delivering. We have been able to look at a range of data which the Senior Team have turned into quality information for year cohorts, subject groups as well as for individuals. This means we can really use data to raise achievement. ICT has greatly helped Governors work in ensuring that the school improvement plan is delivered.

Our Governors have given general and wide support for the school being part of the Technology College initiative and the Technology College programme and saw this as a lever for increasing the amount of ICT in the School. The Head and Senior Team have always used such initiatives as catalysts. The Governors are linked to specific departments where we have been able to give further support to this development. We have enjoyed observing ICT used across the school to enhance teaching and learning. The most marked value to students seems to be providing access to a far broader and richer range of learning resources. It clearly supports my own son's thinking as he can research, retrieve and incorporate up-to-date data into in-depth projects. He has found it helpful for evaluating different perspectives and views as more windows are open giving a wide range of views.

We have supported the Head and leadership team in using ICT in their roles and in ensuring that the administration of the school is facilitated by the judicious use of ICT. We are now beginning to create proper information bases.

The key for successfully introducing ICT at our school was bringing it in across the school to all departments, not treating it as a separate entity. It would be wrong to limit such a valuable way of working. The real challenge is training staff to be equipped and competent enough to take advantage of the new technologies. It is as important for teachers to learn and exploit this as it is for students. In other words I am saying 'Learning together, Achieving together' – the school credo! This learning must be integrated into all staff's professional development.

The other important factor in our successful introduction of ICT has been having the Director of New Technologies as a key member of the leadership team. I think this has been profoundly significant. The high quality of project management, monitoring and evaluation under his direction has been really essential. The appointment of a strong team of co-ordinators to work under his direction has also been vital. Having these co-ordinators in key departmental clusters has pushed down responsibility and has created natural leaders in each area of the school.

■ How can I give a lead?

Check through the SHA IT Policy, set out below (which was drawn up before the term ICT was in common use).

SHA IT Policy

The Secondary Heads Association is strongly committed to continuing high quality education for all. All young people must acquire the key skills of literacy, numeracy and the handling of information through the use of new technology, by the time they reach the age of nineteen. The development of literacy and numeracy will be supported by the good use of IT.

Our excitement in and commitment to new technology is fuelled by our experience of the following using IT:

- opportunities to stimulate intellectual curiosity and to put the fun back into learning;
- enhanced learning opportunities across all areas of the curriculum;
- access to high level concepts by managing complex processes quickly, e.g. Maths calculations and design;
- access to enormous areas of information;
- access to current information in those subjects where information is constantly changing;

■ new opportunities for learning through individualised flexible programmes which provide the right incremental steps;

■ access to interactive learning;

■ opportunities for pupils to communicate and empathise by bridging such artificial barriers as geography, age and culture;

■ access to expert, inspirational 'teachers';

■ greater opportunities for home learning;

■ real scope for community life-long learning;

■ removal of discrimination often linked to race, sex, and disabilities;

■ non-judgmental experience in learning – the machine allows mistakes;

■ excellent presentation of ideas by all.

SHA wants IT to improve and ensure:

■ quality of teaching;

■ quality of resourcing;

■ all young people learning;

■ all young people prepared for positive future roles in society.

Consider the following questions:

Ethical and moral issues relating to IT

Open access to 'skills and information' is power

On entitlement and equality of access

■ How will you involve all students in developing the school's IT ethics policy?

■ How will you ensure that all students have an entitlement access to IT both in and out of lessons?

■ How will you ensure that all students are extended by the use of technology in support of their personal and academic development?

■ What provision have you made to support students who have no home resources?

■ How do you level up teachers' skills for IT so that they can all develop a comparable use of IT over the whole curriculum?

- What is your policy when there are not enough computers or expertise to go round?

On quality and gate-keeping

- Are the ethical and moral issues associated with IT being discussed by pupils and staff?
- Do you want resources to be of assured quality and accuracy – or should pupils have open access and be educated to assess quality of information?
- What is the effect of privacy of access on the present social controls on moral attitudes?
- Is a 'walled garden' approach relevant if pupils have open access at home, or should the school safeguard the rights of parents who would not allow open access at home?
- How would you know that students are accessing areas that are unsuitable or corrupting?
- How do you ensure that students do not access such areas?
- How do you ensure that students exercise their own appropriate discrimination?

Ownership of sources, copyright and confidentiality

- Who owns the information we gather on pupils, staff, parents, governors and others?
- How do we ensure that confidentiality is not breached?
- How do we ensure the confidentiality of data including print-outs?
- For what purpose can we legitimately use information gathered by the school?

MANAGEMENT ISSUES
Leadership

- What is your curriculum vision and how should it impact on your use of IT?
- How will you communicate your vision to colleagues, governors, parents and students?
- How will you translate your leadership vision into practical reality?

■ What impact do you want IT to have on learning and teaching within your institution?

■ What practical outcomes, for students' development, are you expecting from your IT policy?

■ What is your vision of partnership between home/school/local business/local industry?

■ What aspects of IT will enhance a continuous learning process for all which will command support from both school and home?

■ What is your commitment to developing your school as a learning 'hive' where staff and students' intellectual curiosity is enhanced and supported by IT?

■ What is your commitment to education as a continuous life-long process with equality of access for all the school's community?

■ What management arrangements will you make for:
1. development planning;
2. best communication;
3. administration including financial arrangements;
4. learning support;
5. care, repair and maintenance;
6. training;
7. monitoring and evaluation?

Managing the cost

1. Drawing up the specification which should be curriculum-led

■ How do you decide what is fit-for-purpose?

■ Who draws up the specification?

■ How do you ensure your process meets local government regulations?

2. Things not to overlook

■ purchase versus loan costs;

■ staff training costs;

■ software and hardware support costs;

■ insurance costs;

■ on-costs, e.g. telephone/ISDN costs;

■ installation costs.

3. How would you measure value for money?

Integration of IT across the curriculum

Computer rooms

- How do you know that every pupil learns basic skills and has the opportunity to develop further skills?
- Which departments use the computer rooms?
- How easy is the access?
- How varied are the applications used in the IT lessons?

Department computers

- How do you know every pupil learns basic skills and has opportunity to develop further skills?
- Is all the equipment being used?
- Are all departments using IT?
- Who knows what skills are being built up within a year group or department?
- How do you know who is using the computers in the library, resource area, etc?

For the whole school:

- How many people know what is happening across the curriculum?
- How do departments collaborate?
- How are you ensuring equal opportunities for all pupils?

Training

- Have you got the same aims for your staff as for your students?
- Is your whole staff computer literate at a basic level?
- How many IT 'blockers' have you got?
- What initiatives (e.g. report writing, assessment, attendance packages, value-added data) are hampered as result?
- Do you intend to face the hurdle of a fully-trained staff or will you go around the problem?
- Will you use in-house training or cascading?

Many of the issues raised above are covered later in this book, but our response to some of them is summarised here.

■ Student entitlement and equality of access

We have a School Council that is used for both developing and reviewing policy. This allows us to engage with students in discussions, moving to a consensus position on all policies. We have also drawn heavily upon the Scottish Council for Education and Technology February 1996 Information Ethics document. We are committed to creating a safe information environment.

■ Hampstead School Ethical Policy

Hampstead School will follow the Universal Declaration of Human Rights and our commitment to comprehensive schooling:

■ Education shall be directed to the full development of the human personality and to the strengthening of respect for human rights and fundamental freedoms. It shall promote understanding, tolerance and friendship among nations, racial or religious groups, and shall further... the maintenance of peace.

■ All students and staff regardless of race, gender, sexual orientation or social situation are endowed with reason and conscience.

■ All students and staff regardless of race, gender, sexual orientation or social situation have the right to be treated with respect as equals in dignity.

■ All students and staff regardless of race, gender, sexual orientation or social situation must act towards one another in a spirit of sisterhood and brotherhood.

■ All students and staff regardless of race, gender, sexual orientation or social situation have the right to personal privacy unless this infringes on, threatens or harms themselves or others.

■ All students and staff regardless of race, gender, sexual orientation or social situation have the right to freedom of thought, conscience and religion unless this infringes on, threatens or harms others.

■ All students and staff regardless of race, gender, sexual orientation or social situation have the right to express their personal opinions unless these harm others.

Access of all students and staff to information, views and activities must ensure that all the above are observed.

■■■■ **Hampstead School Ethical Policy for ICT**

■ All staff should be fully informed about the new technologies so that they can prevent students from experimenting with unsuitable material.

■ All staff should maintain a friendly but vigilant interest in all users' computer activities.

■ School stand-alone computers and networks must be secure environments so tracing problems is easy.

■ Regular logging needs to be established to identify unexpected uses of programs.

■ Secure areas need to be established which block access to unauthorised others.

■ Students need to be made aware of on-line etiquette, and the dangers of pornography, racism and violence; to be able to be aware of and critically assess bias and distortion, censorship, advertising, pirating, hacking, computer viruses and illegal operations.

■■■■ ICT across the curriculum

We are committed to delivering ICT across the curriculum. This means all students have access to ICT in a wide range of lessons, using ICT for many different purposes. This was recently highlighted by OFSTED as an area of excellence. An important use of computers is for students to prepare records of achievement and CVs. Having a detailed record of their achievements, well presented on disk with easy updating, raises students' self esteem. Students learn to work co-operatively together in many lessons using and sharing computers and this improves their social skills. We regularly use e-mail and video conference links with a school in France. This is a very exciting development and students have to learn to be reliable correspondents. Their social skills are also important when speaking to French students in a more formal environment.

By ensuring that ICT is delivered across the curriculum, we have ICT facilities available across the whole school site. There is also an open-house policy for students before, during and after school where they may come and use departmental and year facilities. We also have a superb Independent Learning Centre which we developed using our first tranche of Technology College money. This has 41 networked PCs which allow students access to a wide range of ICT tools, reference materials and learning software. We also work in some classes with sufficient computers for half the pupils. This allows colleagues to teach half groups while the other half are working independently. All students can apply for their own e-mail address and work can be stored and retrieved easily. This facility is open from 8.00am to 5.00pm currently, but we have plans to extend this considerably when funding becomes available. A few special needs students have ICT written into their statements, but it is not feasible to provide all students with computers and, at the time of writing, only 60% of our students have computer access at home.

We have had training and support on a regular basis delivered internally and there is an ethos in which we learn from each other as well as from students. In 1984, a Year 10 student, Alex Golner, asked to have two days off to attend the Frankfurt Book Fair as his first book on ICT was being launched. That is an extreme example but many of our students who find conventional learning challenging are transformed by using technology. They have no fear. We welcome and exploit their expertise knowing they can also gain valuable social skills by supporting others.

3 Management

Why use ICT for management in school?

ICT builds teams of learners

We have found that training on the job and together makes us all talk about learning how to use ICT effectively. In the past, most staff teams had one computer and shared it and their expertise. We have always worked to spread ICT across all staff and the whole school administration and curriculum.

ICT makes us more efficient

Before having computers in the office, we had a secretary who could not spell. If she made a mistake, she had to type the whole letter or document out again. Record keeping was also laborious, with lots and lots of card files and messy Roneo master sheets. It took ages to communicate or record things.

ICT increases our access to and our use of information and expertise

By using the Internet and e-mail, we can instantly access information across the world. One of our first staff to experience this was a scientist, Thomas William-Powlett, who was a wizard at this. He put up on the Internet some science programmes he had designed and produced. He had responses and ideas sent to him from America and Australia. This opened our eyes to the speed and breadth of the sources of information and support.

The school management staff have never been seen as separate from the teaching staff and, before ICT, used to have to type out worksheets designed by teachers. Now this is not one of their chores. As leaders and managers we have considerable support from the Open University Website for Serving Headteachers, from our Union websites – with the latest information on performance-related pay – as well as from the National Grid for Learning, the DfEE site, QCA, TTA and many others.

ICT improves our communications

Communicating quickly with parents and with all the other educational partners is vital. We are able to offer an up-to-date information line, our website has an interactive facility and we produce a weekly broadsheet, *Hampstead BUZZ*, which carries photos, pictures scanned or digitally downloaded as well as the latest news. Our Year 11 students organised their own 'Year Book' using ICT but we have still some way to go to equal Keith Parry's CD-ROM made by his students in the GNVQ group at Hyde Technology College Tameside. Keith Parry was winner of the Plato Awards (Teaching Awards Trust) in 1999 for the most Creative Use of ICT in a Secondary School.

ICT supports our efforts to improve and change practice

Our School Improvement Plan is a co-operative effort. This relies on very rapid links using ICT and easy access to information from monitoring. Policies can be mulled over and added to easily if a change is only a click away.

ICT allows us to practise what we preach

At Hampstead, we have the slogan 'Learning together, Achieving together'. This is for real! We expect all staff to be learning as much as all the students. This means we want to show students that we are moving into the knowledge and technology age, and learning as we embrace new technologies. We are not saying 'Do as we tell you'. We are saying 'Do as we do' – a far more powerful message.

ICT usually makes life easier

Well, yes, there are crashes and problems (often constant problems), but each is just a challenge and each time we overcome a problem – whether it is the ETHAN virus (we escaped the Love Bug!) or just our inexperience – we learn and improve. For the rest of the time life is far easier. Many of us could never have undertaken challenging further degrees on top of present workloads as leaders and managers running a large and successful school without being able to access information and use word processor and spreadsheets to analyse data. We are able to log into the University of London Institute of Education Library from home or school, wherever we are. On the Internet we can find books needed for doctorate and further degree studies and have details of these e-mailed directly to us.

ICT makes what we do exciting and fun

There is no doubt about the excitement and fun. There is a real sense of achievement when one has produced an excellent Governors' report, incorporated everyone's contributions and sent if off on time with quotes taken from the Internet, illustrations scanned from our students' work, and no spelling mistakes thanks to the spellchecking facility. Interestingly, spellchecks help us become better spellers because they pick up words we may have become blind to mis-spelling. Our latest excitement is using the search for text facility in Word. This has saved hours because none of us is very organised at filing on the computer.

What are the challenges of using ICT?

Crashes

We have all had more than enough of these, and we refer to the worst on pages 26–7. Back-ups are essential and we are now converted to the need to use ZIP discs and to back up onto these regularly. This also ensures you weed out useless files that are just taking up space.

Fear and apprehension

Have a go! Everyone is learning because ICT is constantly changing. It is a bit like sailing – until you try, you are so impressed by those who appear to know lots that it can prevent you from starting. Don't be put off. Even ICT 'boffins' don't know everything, and if they can't explain it to you, then they are not that good!

Information overload

In a recent computer survey, managing to select the right information and then use it was the thing most people, including students, were concerned about. However, cutting and pasting, searching for key words, having the facility to set out the bare bones of a piece of writing and then to fill it in is really helpful. The important thing is to know what key questions you want to research and not to be sidetracked by distractions along the way.

■ Upgradings and costs

Yes, ICT is expensive, but ICT is the one area that keeps on getting cheaper. I bought my first personal computer in 1992. It was an RM notebook with 25 MHZ and 2 Megabytes of memory. It cost £1641.29. One of the authors noted, 'I bought it because it was the same as those we had in school and it meant I would have help from staff and students if I went wrong! My latest computer, bought in 1999, was the same price but with 300 MHZ and 64 Megabytes of memory, as well as CD-ROM and Internet access!'

These days ICT is no longer an option. The Government is beginning to be aware of the importance of providing additional resources to support ICT. The real costs are those of training and technical support because it is not having the computer that is the problem, but it is being able to keep going. Technical support is crucial and it is expensive. But it gives confidence to the first stage teacher and other staff learners.

■ Training

Training is really important, but not all training should take people away from their work. The best is given on the job when the need arises and it can come from students who have no fear or hang ups and are prepared to play until they learn. It can also come from colleagues who are just a little more advanced than you are. This is often the best training because these 'teachers' have only just mastered the difficulty or skill themselves and they will remember the sequencing and the scaffolding you need to do it for yourself.

■ Health risks

There are risks from sitting on ergonomically lethal seating, and from having computers on benching or tables at the wrong height. These problems are best sorted out by seeking the advice of an ergonomist. These days many osteopaths, who usually have to sort out the mess we make of our bodies, are also experienced in this area. Our Site and Services Development Officer was given a new office and desk after we took the good advice from just such a person.

There are useful exercises you can do. It is also sensible to make sure that you are never sitting for too long and that you combine some active work alongside a sedentary period at a computer. This is seldom a problem for teachers! When choosing screens and keyboards, take specialist advice. Most computer firms are now taking this seriously.

Security

The best advice is to shut the door before the horse has bolted! We have always organised security and alarms before we installed any of our ICT. This has saved us a lot of grief. Most of our problems have come from inside or from people subverting the security we have. One stolen lap-top computer was returned when the shop it was offered to opened it up to read on the screen that it was the property of Hampstead School!

ICT as a secondary management tool

We use ICT for handling data to do with all of the following: finance, staff and student records, policies and systems, exam and test results, the curriculum; the timetable; stock records. We also use it to carry out the following operations and presentations: storage, networking, time management.

Data protection

The protection of data is important and is addressed in the following case study. It is a matter of having passwords and restricted access – which is possible if you have someone with the technical expertise to set it up.

Case study 1 – How we store data safely at Hampstead School

Our first nightmares about using ICT became a reality ten years ago. We had been given an out-of-date hardware and software system, bought by the unsuspecting LEA. Basically this system worked for about two years from 1990–92. The day the server crashed will never be forgotten, and it was followed by a major upturn in my learning curve! The server was repaired and made ready for the back-up tape which should have restored our data. When the back-up tape was put in, however, it was found to be corrupted. The further back-ups were also corrupted so in one fell swoop we lost the previous two years of school data and documents.

An ICT software expert took three weeks trying to retrieve the situation, but only managed to save part of our student data. All of our word-processed documents, including the School Improvement Plan and our policies, were irretrievably lost. I was ready to walk out and never come back. However, the LEA paid for all the data to be re-entered and we used this as an opportunity to move forward and to improve what we had done before. We learned to take control of ICT, not to be controlled by ICT. I became an expert and was seconded by the LEA who realised that a users' group was critical for success. I supported other schools to ensure no such disaster occurred again. I gained enormously by linking with other schools and speaking to colleagues who were also developing ICT for management.

▓▓ SIMS

At Hampstead School, we use the personnel module of the Schools Information Management System (SIMS). Here, we can record basic details of all staff: personal information such as name and address as well as details from their work contract including posts held, whether permanent or temporary, job title and salary details. For teachers, this includes the breakdown of points which make up their salary, and details of responsibility allowances and threshold payments. Having got the information on SIMS, we can then pull off analyses of any of these fields of data and any combination – for example, payroll numbers, dates of birth, phone numbers, and car registration numbers. These analyses are invaluable for both the school, the LEA, Governors, and DfEE and Technology College returns. Student data is also held on SIMS.

ICT is valuable in this management task for a number of reasons. You can use the sort function on any field – alphabetical, date of birth, teachers eligible for the threshold or imminently at the threshold. It helps with budgeting because you can find out what spine point each member of staff is on before making any financial calculations. This data and any of the analyses can be exported to spreadsheets and further manipulated – for example, salaries may be linked to scales in order to project salary costs.

Originally our student data was held on NOVA-T along with the timetable data. We outgrew this system because we ran out of fields to record the ever-increasing number of details. Transferring student data to SIMS presented some problems because three per cent of the data for 1300 students was not held correctly and required us to make individual time-consuming alterations.

Confidentiality and data protection are very important issues and we address these by limiting access to key managers. The SIMS software allows us to set up individual access levels for users. Some users have no access, while others have a read-only facility. Editing access is very tightly restricted and passwords are critical.

▮▮▮ Advice for others who are not quite at this stage

- Start small and build on early successes, thus continually increasing your confidence.
- Have a go.
- Network with others.
- Remember that we are all human and communicate in layperson terms to develop understanding and knowledge.
- Never forget to back up.
- Always test that your back-up works before it is too late.
- Choose hardware and software you have seen operating in the way you would like to use it.
- Only skim-read software brochures and always ask to be put in touch with a comparable user.

▮▮▮ How can ICT assist us in the production of documents and publications?

The major problems with all documentation are printing and updating. We will always want some hard copies but the use of linked on-line access means that huge documents like our 300-page *Staff Guide* can be available to all and updated regularly. No one can say they have lost it!

▮▮▮ School brochure

The brochure was originally printed out of school but, with improved colour photocopying, we will be able to update it and run off just sufficient for our needs so it is never out of date. We already have the whole brochure on our website.

▮▮▮ Weekly news bulletin – *Hampstead Buzz*

Without the use of a digital camera, scanner and publisher formatting, this regular and much appreciated publication would be impossible to produce. Copy comes in dribs and drabs, and any visitor or exciting activity is news. Putting it all in the *Hampstead Buzz* has resulted in the creation of a fascinating record of the daily life of the school. Using photos scanned or directly added from a digital camera enhances the immediacy. We found lots was happening which people wanted recorded instantly, knowing it would be out and publicised within a week. The bulletin is also placed on the website. However, our website is still rather behind so pupil post is the most direct method of distribution until we can get the technical support hours or – better – we learn to add it to the website ourselves!

How can we use ICT to analyse our examination results and use this to raise teachers' expectations and students' achievement?

'*The careful analysis of a wide range of data on examination performance is used to set targets for departments, identify areas for improvement and plan developments.*'

'*Good use is made of assessment information to support the identification of special needs.*'

(Short OFSTED Report 2000, Hampstead School)

Case study 2 – ICT in examination administration at Hampstead School

The responsibilities and duties attached to the position of examination secretary have changed and expanded so rapidly in the last decade that it is now unimaginable that the work could be done without the use of ICT. Before the nineties, the job involved entering students for CSE, O-level and A-level examinations once a year. Fewer students attempted many fewer examinations with mainly one, usually local, examination board. Interest in the results of these examinations was minimal and confined to the school; no outside body took much interest at all. Teachers wasted little time searching for different examination syllabuses to improve results. Examination secretaries rarely had changes to deal with and all entries were done by filling in forms.

The advent of GCSEs a decade ago resulted not only in an explosion in the numbers of students taking examinations, but in a much wider range of subjects being taken, usually with a multiplicity of boards.

Examination secretaries have now to face the challenge of meeting all the complex entry regulations and deadlines the different boards demand. Students who previously took four or five CSEs now enter for eight or nine GCSEs. The subjects are taken at different levels (tiers) and may have several different components, including coursework. Some examinations require registration in Year 10 if they are modular, and entry at different times of the year. The introduction of modular A-levels in many subjects has meant an enormous amount of extra administration because modules are available at different times of the year and many students wish to resit modules to improve their grades.

In order to make it possible to administer these vastly more complicated entries, the examination boards themselves began to make available software to aid communication with them. At Hampstead School, programmes from our local examination board were used. Entry was by computer printout, later to be followed by disks. The novelty of completing the entry on the computer and finally 'putting it to bed' by transferring it to disk instead of filling in enormous sheets of carbonised paper was a delight never to be forgotten. The advantages were truly brought home when, one year, the entire network crashed only hours before the final transfer was to be made. The only way out was to spend the next week working full time together with a secretary doing the entry by hand!

In order to keep track of the increased entry, examination boards demanded many details with codes designed to differentiate the different tiers. Personal details, including candidate numbers, have to be supplied together with the eight or nine subjects for each student. Thankfully the ICT department at Camden LEA had also started to become interested because the examination results of schools were about to leave the small world of their own school environments and enter the public domain. The LEA realised that if results were to be scrutinised by the DfEE and the world at large, so making schools and LEAS accountable, then a reliable and consistent approach was needed in all schools across the borough. They set about developing their own system with some consultants but soon discovered that it was more expedient to purchase commercial software that had already incorporated analyses of results. All schools in the Authority were provided with the software, training and back-up.

The situation today is ever more complicated and again only manageable using ICT. The introduction of modular exams in many subjects has meant that each candidate is allocated a 13-digit unique candidate number which must stay with the candidate and not be allocated to anyone else. The examination boards use these to keep track of modules which have been banked for later use. For a large school where Year 11 contains over 200 GCSE candidates and Year 13 contains 100 students taking A-levels, as well as Years 10 and 12 taking modules, there is vast amount of information to be communicated both to the board and to the staff and students. Using ICT means that staff are able to easily make their entries, and each student can have their own individual entry slip to cross-check. This eliminates many costly mistakes. When the entries are confirmed as correct, each student receives an individual timetable. Using ICT also makes the detection of timetable clashes very simple.

In addition to the above use of ICT, all information is transmitted to and from the examination boards via electronic data interchange (EDI). Examination results can be downloaded the day before they are to be released to the students. This allows the printing and collating of results for students and staff to be ready in good time and makes them easily accessible to both at a stressful time when important decisions have to be made on the strength of the results. With the advent of league tables there is far more interest in how good the results are and, on the day they arrive, the LEA, local and national newspapers, radio and television are all standing by to receive the analyses by fax by midday. This would be impossible without ICT.

On a day-to-day basis, examination invigilation has been made a great deal simpler by using ICT to publish an examination timetable together with details of rooms and invigilators. It is an aid to management of the daily cover. The analyses produced by ICT can be a powerful tool for the senior management to analyse strengths and weaknesses in different subjects. It is easy to collate, compare and contrast the results of different members of a department or one department with another. This is a controversial area and necessarily needs to be managed sensitively, but the ease with which this sort of information can be generated by using ICT means that it is bound to be used more and more as a tool to enable the sharing of good practice and to improve results.

The future looks set to rely even more on ICT. With the advent of the new AS/A2 system there will be huge increases again in the numbers of students taking extra subjects and being examined at the end of Year 12.

How can we best use ICT for budgeting and finance?

'Financial planning is very thorough and the principles of best value are used when allocating resources.'   (OFSTED 2000, Hampstead School)

■ Case study 3 – Using ICT for budgeting and finance

To start with, I use spreadsheets to plan. The first thing we have to do is analyse existing salary costs and make projections for curriculum and timetable changes, for example for our new curriculum post 16. I can link basic salary details and changes to specific salaries. I have a spreadsheet for the staff and a spreadsheet with the salaries. I then link these by the use of formulae which allows me to link one example and then copy this linkage across all the data. I use look-up tables I have previously prepared to assist. These tables can be easily updated and then that data is automatically transferred across. This enables us to do the 'What if?' scenarios.

I use the Research Machines module called Cash Accounts. This is designed for use by school staff rather than for businesses. It is tailor-made for schools because it is simple and straightforward, using everyday language rather than accounting terms. It is easy to enter data such as our income and expenditure and budget allocations. Users can be given access levels to specific areas, such as batching income – where one person enters the income. This can then be authorised by another. It is like putting data into a temporary file. It is an easy way to please the auditors because there is monitoring and two people can check. It speeds up entry because amendments are easy. If you do something, there is always a reversal option. There is always an audit trail to track data entries identifying which user entered each transaction.

ICT is valuable in this management task because it allows us all to have instant, accurate, updated information on our expenditure, earmarked expenditure and forecasts set against the formally agreed set budget. This means we can ensure we are keeping within accept-able limits. We would not be able to deliver to the requirements of a locally managed school without this.

There have also been challenges. I remember one of the first salary spreadsheets I did that did not work out. A little knowledge can be a dangerous thing. It is essential to know approximately the results one would expect and to check carefully that every step has been taken correctly. Simple mistakes like an omission can invalidate everything. But simple mistakes are simply corrected.

■ Advice for others who are not quite at this stage:

- Don't rush into using new software.
- Take time to plan with others (particularly those who have to enter data) what you want to achieve.

■ Make sure you know approximately what order of result you would expect.

■ ICT is not something that happens only in the administration sector. Make sure it is a joint venture with teachers, other staff and ICT specialists as well as specialist administration staff.

■ Make sure on-site technical support is available.

■ Persevere because, when authorities want data for the umpteenth time, it makes such a difference to be able to pull off data quickly.

How can we best use ICT to assist us in curriculum modelling, planning and timetabling?

Case study 4 – ICT and the timetabler

Times past

From time to time, I am told by teachers who remember such things that there used to exist a large plastic board which contained hundreds of little slots. This object took pride of place in the office of teacher in charge of the curriculum. By all accounts this person withdrew from the life of the school into a state of purdah between April and July each year. Few people caught a glimpse of him or her during this time but those who did told of disturbing sights of a huddled figure staring for hours on end at the huge plastic edifice, of thousands of plastic pegs each labelled with inexplicable numbers. Occasionally, rumours circulated about the board having fallen to the ground spilling a plethora of pegs to the floor, leaving a scene resembling an earthquake in an Early Learning Centre.

Eventually, after months of deliberation, gallons of coffee and minimal consultation, the office door creaked open and a figure emerged clutching a sheaf of paper and heading off in the direction of the specialist printers. Finally, on a day in mid-July with the car engine running, the timetabler would post an Al sheet behind a sealed glass frame and make off towards Provence with all the acceleration of a drag racer.

I am no silicon son, but when I was first charged with writing the timetable for a large comprehensive school, I couldn't envisage completing the job without significant use of ICT.

▇▇▇ Times present

The very processes of staff audits, curriculum planning, scheduling and allocating rooms require the interactive skills that are so easily accomplished with ICT. The days when the timetable was finished, posted and forgotten are long since over. In a large modern school the timetable is an organic document constantly evolving, changing, improving and rotating, not just during its conception but during its currency. The use of ICT gives this flexibility and, of course, allows everyone in the school instant access to the most up-to-date version.

The most commonly anticipated problem of e-timetabling is that you can't step back and look at the global view, as you can with mechanical methods. This is because you can only peer through windows at small parts of the timetable at any one time. Of course, a larger monitor and smaller fonts allow you to see more, but you are never going to see the whole structure. Once you get used to this it presents no problem as long as you are able to trust the program not to double schedule teachers or classes.

Unlike the timetabler of old it would be impossible to create a timetable now without close consultation with curriculum managers. By working on the timetable in manageable segments, the system allows constant consultation by being able to print out departmental timetables, which can be shared with Heads of Department. The timetabler can be working on one chapter whilst a previous chapter is with a department. This sort of consultation allows for checks and balances at all stages of the timetable construction and prevents early errors necessitating complete unravelling of the timetable.

A good Head of Department will also consult with their staff. Hence everyone feels empowered within the overall process and the timetabler is less likely to get a queue of disappointed teachers in September.

It is crucial for the timetable to be part of the school management software. It must link in with databases that carry information about staff and students so that the whole package can provide instant information. It then becomes possible to immediately communicate changes, such as carousel-movement room changes and changes in staffing so that the timetable is constantly up to date.

A computerised timetable package will also allow you to print student timetables and deal with daily staff absences whilst simultaneously keeping records. Anything that saves work gets my vote.

How can we use ICT to assist us in improving attendance and punctuality?

'The careful analysis of a wide range of data on attendance patterns, is used to set targets for departments, identify areas for improvement and plan developments.'
(OFSTED 2000, Hampstead School)

Case study 5 – Using ICT to analyse attendance and punctuality

I started using ICT at university so I could wordprocess my essays and use Excel to produce a few charts. The university ran training sessions and provided back-up technical support. For most of the time, though, I taught myself because I was producing real documents I actually wanted. I remember one problem I kept having – the INSERT key was sometimes switched on by accident and I found that as fast as I typed it kept eating the words!

At Hampstead School we use an old DOS-based system for attendance, which I find quite easy once you know how. It's just like a tree with all the different branches growing off it. Our Technical Support Manager showed me a few things and then I skim-read the manual to pick out what I needed. Then it was just trial and error.

Basically each teacher has a BROMCOM folder which is an electronic register – really a mini computer that can transmit the data over a radio link. This information is fed into a central computer based in our administration centre. Teachers can input the following for every student:

- present or absent;

- unauthorised and different authorised absences;

- number of minutes late.

Teachers can access a history of data for each student in their class or tutor group to assist in understanding patterns and problems. Folders can also be used to provide a central alert if there is an intruder or serious problem. Teachers can even e-mail each other!

My job is analysing and updating data, for example, validation and authorisations of attendance. I can provide detailed analyses for individual students, classes, years and teachers. The system also works out percentages of attendance and punctuality.

ICT is valuable in this management task because accurate data can immediately be passed on to staff, students and parents. The computer does all the analyses accurately and tables come ready prepared with summaries at the bottom. Blank registers and certificates of attendance can also be provided.

The major problem is that this is an old DOS-based system, although it can be upgraded at a cost. It is not very user-friendly in its original form, particularly when producing things like certificates which look very drab. It is possible to transfer basic data into a Word document but the only way of doing this without a manual stage is to scan the data and then insert this into a Word-formatted document. If staff want data altered centrally, in the light of subsequent information, it has to be done on the central computer. Teachers can update themselves but they need to learn how to do this. Regular training and familiarisation is important.

Advice for others who are not quite at this stage:

- As a starting point, look at the useful map diagrams in the manual.
- Sit and play around with the system before starting to use it for real.
- Do ask for advice and support if you are stuck.
- Use the help line.

How can we use ICT to assist with cover for absent colleagues?

Case study 6 – Using ICT for cover

We have been using the Nova-T program to help us manage staff cover for about five years. Before that we had a really cumbersome paper with carbon copies approach, which was extremely difficult to alter when, inevitably, someone would ring up and the whole cover schedule for the day might need changing. We had also given an undertaking to our local unions that teachers would be treated fairly and a definitive record of how many covers everybody had done would be kept. Before using Nova-T this required us to keep a handwritten log and, on occasions, this was not 100% accurate.

The brilliant thing about the Nova-T program is that it allows a group of us to take turns in managing fairly and efficiently what can be one of the most dreadful daily chores in a secondary school. The program is easy to use and even a novice can pick it up during a week of practice, with someone a little more experienced to act as a guide and support if there is a problem. As many copies of the cover schedule as needed can be printed, and the cover can be analysed by teacher, department or tutor group as well as give significant information on teacher attendance.

How can we use ICT for the School Improvement Plan?

'Developments are planned thoughtfully and evaluated carefully. It is a reflective school that recognises the challenges facing it and exploits them to the benefit of its pupils. There is a positive ethos and a strong commitment to school improvement and raising standards. Equality of opportunity underpins all decisions taken.'

(OFSTED 2000, Hampstead School)

The first School Development Plan we produced was a vast tome. It was produced using a wordprocessing package in the Deputy Head's office as she was the only person with her own computer – an AppleMac which was not compatible with anything else. This meant we were reliant on the Deputy, Andrea Berkeley, now Head of Preston Manor School, for putting this vast tome together. It took so long that it was out of date before we published it. Now, our essential sheet of Key Objectives with named responsible people can be circulated easily. And, as each Department and Year Team have their own computers, everything, including formats for presenting their own linked plans, is on disk or on the system so it is easy to produce and easy to update. Most important it is easy to use.

Case study 7 – ICT for department development and improvement planning

There are many interconnections between drama and ICT. As the Drama Department at Hampstead School, we have had numerous opportunities to take advantage of the outstanding opportunities offered by the development of ICT provision. As Head of Drama, I have also found this school's spirit of enterprise and ICT provision extremely helpful in planning for improvement in the following areas:

1. cultivating a spirit of partnership;
2. curriculum development;
3. assessing students;
4. developing technical skills;
5. production work.

1. Cultivating a spirit of partnership

Hampstead's ICT development has been characterised by the school's commitment to excellence through partnerships. It seems that the work in ICT, which has spread across each of the departments, can be seen as a microcosm for all that we should strive for in the school's development. It has also encouraged me to consider more integrated approaches to learning and this has empowered me to develop further cross-curricular conversations. I like the fact that the rationales for ICT development have been matched with actual improvements every step of the way. Obviously, different departments have developed in response to these developments at different times and this practice has been communicated to the staff at key training sessions. So, for example, I have learned a great deal from the work that the Geography Department has shared on assessment procedures and this has helped in this department's development. A spirit of partnership has both informed and resulted from the development of ICT provision. This has encouraged me to share aspects of the Drama Department's approach to teaching and learning, in one case on the development of presentation skills, with staff in a training session. Obviously, this has been important in raising the profile of this department, generating further discussions in all departments (including ours) about different approaches, and highlighting key areas for our action plan relating to high quality teaching.

2. Curriculum development

Increased ICT development has enabled us to plan a range of opportunities to enhance students' learning in many different ways. As a department, we have created an improvement plan that incorporates ICT skills at each key stage. So, for example, we now incorporate the teaching of scriptwriting in Year 7 through the use of a simple networked form. However, it is a reframing of the school's approach to independent study which has had the most impact on the department's improved approach to setting up tasks. This has inspired us to incorporate independent learning tasks and methodologies relating to ICT for each key stage. For example, we now set up our Year 9 students with a research brief relating to their study of Didactic Theatre and Bertolt Brecht. In Year 10 we are planning to give each of our students a disk to compile the compulsory written coursework, which will allow us to review and refine the work in an area which some of our most talented students find extremely challenging.

3. Assessing students

Formative assessment is vital to the development of work in drama and can often redirect the course of a lesson. Part of my department's improvement plan relates to the way in which questions can be used for reflection to support target setting and further learning. New initiatives relating to formative assessment and review, and also a new networked formative system, is another way in which ICT has helped to focus the department on improving our systems relating to how we assess students' learning in drama.

4. Developing technical skills

The introduction and use of new equipment has heightened my awareness of the importance of giving staff and students the opportunity to present work of the highest quality. In terms of long-term development planning, the refurbishment of the library has reminded me of the importance of a top-quality learning environment. Therefore, we are currently seeking ways to improve existing spaces and also generate income to develop our technical equipment further. In terms of curriculum planning, this is leading to the instigation of a new Performing Arts course next year.

5. Production work

Our current production is a newly commissioned work. *The Road to Mandalay* has been written by John McGrath and the music has been composed by Rick Lloyd. The play is written as a celebration of the Universal Declaration of Human Rights. Therefore, it has required students to research a range of topics, from the United Nations to specific countries and significant people who feature in the play – Patrice Lumumba, for example. The arrival of our new networked computer at the start of the rehearsal process was extremely timely! Many of the students and staff involved in the production have used it for research and also to generate resources such as images and display material for the play. The experience has shown me the importance of using ICT to support all extra-curricular activities in the future and we will endeavour to do so.

How can we use ICT for assessment and target setting?

Targets in the past should have been more precisely called goals. We did not have the data or the means to predict so we were unable to set ambitious but achievable goals. In order to focus on raising achievements, we set almost impossible goals like 100% staying-on rates post 16. This we have nearly achieved and 92% stayed on in our Sixth and parallel Sixths/Colleges in 1999. Using ICT and simple baseline data it has been possible for us to analyse how our students are performing and to predict their future performance. This then allows us to set realistic targets for Government purposes, although goals move us further.

Assessment is not an end in itself. It is not something we should see as imposed upon us for outside purposes, but is a tool for the deeper and more effective education of our students and management of our organisation. ICT makes it much easier to use assessment and not be used by it.

 ## Case study 8 – The use of ICT for assessment

At Hampstead School, we have been using ICT in various ways to help with the recording and reporting of assessment data for some time. We used to use a DOS-based profiling system running on an old 186 PC, which read in codes from OMR sheets and built student profiles from statement banks. This was abandoned for a number of reasons. The system was time-consuming and difficult to administer – staff had to know which codes triggered which statements and it was all too easy to create rather ambiguous or meaningless reports.

Like many schools we use spreadsheets to produce a wide range of summary information, using baseline assessments (Key Stage 2 SATs, London Reading Tests, Cognitive Ability Tests) and public examinations (Key Stage 3 SATs, GCSEs, GNVQs and A-levels). Graphs are produced to make the information simpler to analyse, so that trends over time can be seen and comparisons can be made. The school has also used YELLIS and ALIS to help predict outcomes at GCSE and A-level, which are used at individual, departmental and whole-school levels to assist in target-setting.

We are just starting to use the SIMS module Assessment Manager to store and analyse important data. Any type of grade or mark can be entered into this program, either manually or using an import feature. Grades can be given a numeric equivalent so that they can be used to make comparisons. Marks and grades can be reproduced on a report for parents, students or staff, and can be linked to statement banks. If used in an ongoing way, a complete record of a student's achievements can be built over time so that progress can be tracked and monitored. We are using Assessment Manager to store marks/ grades of information such as: effort, achievement, behaviour, homework, presentation, national curriculum level, estimated GCSE grade, coursework and exam results.

One of the most useful features of Assessment Manager is the statistical analysis tool, which allows us to take prior attainment data (for example Key Stage 3 SATs levels) for a particular cohort and correlate it with current performance (for example GCSE expected grade). This helps us to single out those students who are performing well beyond expectations for the group and give them praise and encouragement. It also allows us to identify underachieving students who can be targeted for additional support.

We want to use output data, for example, (National Curriculum levels, GCSE expected grades, etc.), in order to build statement banks containing targets that are formative rather than summative in nature. For example, if a student is currently working at Level 4 in Maths, it is quite useful to them to be given targets for how they can reach Level 5. In the near future, we will be working as a whole-school in order to identify these targets, which are likely to be very focused on skills (rather than content).

Using Assessment Manager, over time we will build up a huge archive of assessment data that will not only allow us to monitor student progress, but also the performance of individual subjects and departments. This information will also enable us to produce examination chances graphs for each subject, based on the school's previous performance.

The use of assessment data to compare departmental performance is clearly a potentially controversial management tool. It is vital that such information is handled carefully and not used as a means of undermining individual staff. We have learned some lessons over the extent to which such data should be made 'public' within the school, and we now prefer to share this information in confidential line management meetings with individual Heads of Department. Of course, there is a certain amount of comparative performance data that will inevitably become generally known, for example, individual subjects' exam results against national averages. This data cannot and should not be ignored, but it needs to be used sensitively and positively for school improvement.

On a more technical note, the sheer difficulty in manually entering data accurately should not be underestimated (someone has to do it!). We frequently make data-entry mistakes, despite careful checks, which lead to incorrect summaries being published. The more data that is entered, the more mistakes will slip through the net. The only solution is to put things right quickly, acknowledging the fault and apologising for any misrepresentation.

Another challenge for us is to find time to properly share individual assessment information with the people concerned. Such data needs talking through so that decisions about what it means and what needs to be done about it can be taken. This applies equally at the whole-school or departmental level when making management decisions, and also at the individual level when helping students to progress and improve.

▬▬ ■ Advice for others who are not quite at this stage:

- Think about the sort of assessment data that is going to be useful to the range of people concerned: students, parents, teachers, Governors, the LEA, the DfEE.

- Be clear about the different ways such data can be used, e.g. summatively, formatively.

- Find time to talk through assessment data properly with the people it concerns.

- Check data as carefully as possible for accuracy, but be prepared for mistakes to be made.

- Do not be too quick to draw conclusions about individual teachers or students from statistical analyses. An individual teacher can be shown to be 'adding value' to one class, but not another. Similarly, an individual student may be exceeding expectations in one subject, but underachieving in another.

- Be extremely careful about the ways in which comparative data on departmental performance is shared with staff. It cannot be ignored, but it needs sensitive handling.

How can we use ICT for quality control: monitoring and evaluation?

Almost all the analyses we do are facilitated by the use of ICT. The first facility is using the computer as a wordprocessor to produce papers. The huge value of the drafting and cut and paste facilities is that they allow us to think and amend as we go along. Excel analyses and graphical representations also make a huge difference.

We have realised that there is so much to be monitored and evaluated that we must select what we are to do and prioritise it against School Improvement Plan issues, and in turn, the Statement of Intent. Below is our monitoring schedule for 1999/2000. This kind of detailed monitoring and analysis would be impossible to carry out without the use of ICT by all parties.

System monitoring and evaluation at Hampstead School raising the achievement levels of all students 1998/2001, as set out in the School Improvement Plan

Each month, named Senior Executive Members will co-ordinate with key leaders a rigorous series of investigations using departmental and year analyses, lesson observations, interviews and questionnaires to collect evidence related to the key questions set out below. Written findings and agreed follow-up action will be presented to the Governors, Quality Assurance Committee, staff, students and parents. This follows the whole-school policy on Monitoring, Evaluation and Action-Planning that was put in place to meet the 1996 OFSTED brief to continue to develop monitoring. This is on top of the routine monitoring, evaluation and target setting which each Leader and team would expect to do. This is monitoring our School Improvement Targets for 1998/2001.

Month	Key Questions	Senior Executive Co-ordinator
September	What do parents and students think of Hampstead School?	Tamsyn Imison
October	How are our students performing at the end of Key Stages 3, 4 and 5 compared with students in comparable schools?	Andy Knowles / Phil Taylor Heather Daulphin / Helen Kidd Mark Southworth / Robin Trowman
November	Who are our under-achieving students? Who are our gifted students?	Andy Knowles / Phil Taylor Helen Kidd / Heather Daulphin
December	Is marking consistent with our assessment and marking policy in all years?	Mark Southworth / Robin Trowman with Heads of Department / Heads of Year
January	Do students and parents understand what levels students have reached, in each subject?	Andy Knowles / Phil Taylor Helen Kidd / Heather Daulphin
February	Have all Subject Leaders been trained to observe and give feedback to their colleagues?	Mark Southworth / Robin Trowman
March	Are Tutors developing their roles supported effectively by their Heads of Year?	Heather Daulphin / Helen Kidd
May	Is a coherent and effective praise system in place for all students?	Heather Daulphin / Helen Kidd
June	Has a new curriculum and structure for delivery been put in place for September 2000?	Mark Southworth / Robin Trowman
July	Have all Departments carried out their action plans to raise the achievement of all under-performing groups?	Andy Knowles / Phil Taylor Helen Kidd / Heather Daulphin
August	Have the SIMS targets set for this academic year been achieved?	Tamsyn Imison

Hampstead School Whole Staff Questionnaire January 1999

This questionnaire will give us valuable information and help us make the school a better place for you to work in. We are looking at support, flexibility, responsibility, standards, rewards, clarity and team commitment. Thank you for taking the time to answer this. *(? = Uncertain)*

Questions	Responses
Please indicate gender & ethnicity.	F – 18 M – 10
Please indicate level of responsibility e.g. DHOD scale 3	1 – 5, 2 – 4, 3 – 9, 4 – 6, 5 – 1
Would you like more support from the Senior Executive?	No – 10, Yes – 18, Unspecified – 12, Pupil management – 3, Consistency – 2, Feedback – 1
Would you like more support from your HOD?	No – 24 (10 commenting on good/excellent support). Yes – 4 (1 each noting communications, more contact)
Would you like more support from the Department team?	Yes – 5, No – 23
Would you like more support from your HOY?	Yes – 3 (1 – pupil behaviour), No – 24
Would you like more support from your line manager?	Yes – 1 each departmentally, Sometimes – 4, On pupil behaviour – 1, No – 23
Are your professional needs being addressed?	Yes – 15, Not entirely/unsure – 4, No response – 4, No one's asked – 1, IT training – 1, Want more contact time – 1

Questions	Please answer the questions below with regard to your main operational team.	Please answer the questions below with regard to the whole school.
Are there unnecessary internal rules and procedures?	Yes – 1, Some – 2, Procedures – 1, No – 21	Yes – 5, Courses – 1, Procedures – 1, No – 11
Is it easy to get new ideas accepted?	Yes – 27, Usually – 1, No – 0	Yes – 12, Sometimes – 6, No – 5, KS4 – 1
Do you feel you have to work against unnecessary internal constraints?	Yes – 2, No – 26	Yes – 10, No – 16
Are you encouraged to take calculated risks based on your own judgement?	Yes – 23, No – 0	Yes – 26, No – 0 not school's fault
Are you given the opportunity to learn from the success or failure of your own efforts?	Yes – 26, Often – 1, Not always – 1	Yes – 18, No – 3 ? – 2

Questions	Responses	
	Please answer the questions below with regard to your main operational team.	Please answer the questions below with regard to the whole school.
Are appropriate tasks delegated to you?	Yes – 25, Mostly – 2, No – 1, ? – 1	Yes – 25, Mostly – 1 No – 1, Too many – 1
Is improving performance emphasised?	Yes – 27, ? – 1, No – 0	Yes – 26, ? – 1, It depends – 1
Are realistic but challenging targets set?	Yes – 26, Usually – 2, No – 0	Yes – 25, Usually – 2, Too many initiatives – 1
Can you participate in review and target setting?	Yes – 28, No – 0	Yes – 26, Usually – 2, No – 0
Are you given feedback on target accomplishment?	Yes – 26, No – 1, Rarely – 1	Yes – 24, No – 4
Are rewards and encouragement given more than criticism and punishment to students?	Yes – 22, No – 2, Equally – 2	Yes – 19, No – 3, Unsure – 3
Are rewards and encouragement given more than criticism and punishment to colleagues?	Yes – 19, No – 4, Equally – 1	Yes – 16, No – 6, ? – 1
Do you receive regular balanced feedback on how you are doing?	Yes – 15, No – 4, Want more – 4	Yes – 7, No – 10, ? – 1
Is good performance seen to lead to increased opportunities for development?	Yes – 15, No – 5, ? – 3	Yes – 12, No – 5, ? – 3
Do you have a clear idea of what is expected of you?	Yes – 25, No – 1	Yes – 20, No – 3, ? – 1
Do you understand how you personally contribute to the vision and targets of the team/school?	Yes – 26, No – ?, ? – 2	Yes – 20, No – 3, ? – 3
Are the policies, procedures and lines of authority and accountability clear and understood by you?	Yes – 23, No – 2	Yes – 18, No – 5, ? – 2 Some policies don't work
Do you feel proud of belonging to your team/school?	Yes – 26, No – 2 Not as I once did – 1	Yes – 20, Mostly – 2, Nil – 4
Do you co-operate with others to achieve team/school targets?	Yes – 28, No – 0	Yes – 27, No – 1
Are differences of opinion valued?	Yes – 27, No – 1	Yes – 14, No – 3, ? – 7
Does unhelpful conflict get resolved?	Yes – 18, Not always – 0 No – 1, None yet – 1	Yes – 12, No – 3 Not always – 7

Please add any comments you feel would be helpful.

(*Staff contributed the following*:)

■ Difficult to be in a small department.

■ Each dept/year seems to function well but seems in isolation a lot of the time. Can we work more as a whole school rather than in separate teams?

■ SMT and Head too quick to criticise and undermine staff. SMT not good at opening up channels of communication so staff can be left in the dark.

■ Discipline policy should be reviewed in light of changing intake.

■ Whole-class learning is being disrupted by a small number of pupils and the systems do not deal with this so the learning of others is seriously affected – there must be consistency.

■ We should have a consistent policy on behaviour including seating, and have consistently high expectations of all pupils re behaviour in class and attitude to learning – it can be done.

■ Atmosphere among staff and pupils is friendly – mutual respect is of the utmost importance, thus for me coming to school is a pleasure, learning new things daily and receiving my reward from the students.

■ I haven't been here long but I am very happy in this school and my department is excellent.

■ Having joined in Sept I have joined a busy vibrant dept and have had plenty of support and opportunities.

■ I feel the admin team are much more supported now by the rest of the staff.

■ The admin team felt very supported as result of encouraging open and frank communications with all concerned.

■ We should pool resources more for pastoral management.

■ I believe 99.9% of staff are doing their best but there are conflicts of role and we need time to catch up with each other and reconcile differences.

4 ICT as a tool for active learning

'*Wherever it is possible, let the student be active rather than passive. This is one of the secrets of making education a happiness rather than a torment.*'
(Russell, 1926, p. 203)

Learning is not always viewed as an active, lifelong pursuit. Many still see schools as a place for passive knowledge transmission – like going to the petrol station to be filled up with fuel. This is a damaging and depressing outlook, because it absolves the learner from any responsibility for their own learning and it turns the school into a place of coercion. This chapter sets out to show that ICT can promote active learning, with reference to several different theories of teaching and learning.

It is the active nature of working with ICT that makes it a powerful tool for learning, and a wide variety of different activities are possible due to its nearly infinite flexibility. Seymour Papert, creator of the educational programming language LOGO, has made great claims for computers in this respect. His inspiration was the enjoyment of playing with toy gear systems as a child: 'gears, serving as models, carried many otherwise abstract ideas into my head' (Papert, 1980, p. vi). He finds his experiences with gears in tune with Piaget's theories of cognitive development, which emphasise active learning. However, he departs from Piaget in one major respect – he identifies an affective aspect to his learning: 'I fell in love with the gears' (Papert, 1980, p. viii). It is Papert's hope that the computer, as the universal machine, can do for others what the gears did for him, both cognitively and affectively.

The influence of feelings on learning is central to the work of Goleman (1995, p. 95) who has described the 'power of emotion to guide effective effort'. The enthusiasm with which most students approach all forms of ICT is frequently observed and commented upon by teachers and is backed-up by research (Cox, 1997). This indicates how this not-so-new technology can still captivate the imagination and motivate learning.

ICT as scaffolding

Hand in hand with active learning goes supportive teaching. Tharp and Gallimore (1988) have usefully equated teaching with 'assisted performance', building on the ideas of Vygotsky. They define assisted performance as 'what a child can do with help, with the support of the environment, of others and of the self' (Tharp and Gallimore, 1988, p. 45). Essentially, the difference between unassisted and assisted performance is what Vygotsky described as the 'Zone of Proximal Development' (ZPD). In Figure 1, the shift from assisted to unassisted performance (and beyond) is summarised, including ideas from Vygotsky, Wertsch, Bruner and Rogoff as set out by Tharp and Gallimore (1988). The diagram shows the four stages of the ZPD:

1. performance assisted by others;
2. performance assisted by self;
3. unassisted performance;
4. de-automisation.

The fourth stage recognises that learning is not a 'once and for all' activity. Mastery of particular skills and concepts can become 'de-automised' by lack of use so that some form of assistance becomes necessary. The process of learning, in terms of the ZPD, is therefore a repetitive cycle. When moving through the ZPD the learner can be characterised first as a spectator, then as a participant as assistance is proffered and accepted – a process Bruner described as 'handover'.

The role of the teacher or 'assistant' is to structure learning situations, providing what is often referred to as 'scaffolding' for the learner. ICT can form an integral part of the scaffolding, by enabling the learner to participate more actively in the learning process. Furthermore, the computer itself can become 'an active partner in the children's learning, giving them important feedback which encourages them to review their decisions' (Cook and Finlayson, 1999, p. 95). At the point when unassisted performance is achieved, skills are internalised and automatised, and any further assistance is usually disruptive and irritating to the learner.

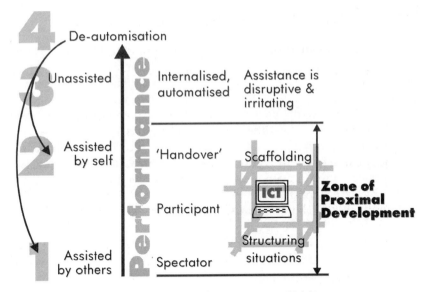

Figure 1 ICT as a tool for active learning – scaffolding

The case study below describes a Science activity in which active learning with ICT, combined with supportive teaching, provided students with a virtual means of exploring and understanding important Science concepts that would not have been possible with real equipment. ICT becomes what Smart (1996, p. 46) has described as a 'catalyst', allowing 'the learning situation to develop a dynamic of its own'.

■ Case study 9 – Science

We are lucky enough to have a dedicated computer suite in our science block – 21 multimedia machines connected to the school Intranet (and relatively small classes of 21 students). It was my second lesson in a row in the suite with my Year 8 (KS3) Science class. At the time we were in the middle of the 'Electricity' topic, and in the previous lesson I had set a graded series of problem-solving exercises using the 'Crocodile Clips' electronics program. These had the dual purpose of giving the class practice in using the program interface (drawing wires and placing components can be quite tricky initially) and reinforcing some of the practical work we had done previously on simple circuits.

The tasks started off simply and got progressively more complex:

- Using two batteries and two bulbs, make both bulbs light up.

- Using two batteries and two bulbs, make both bulbs light up brightly.

- Using two batteries, two bulbs and a switch, make both bulbs turn on and off together.

- Using two batteries, two bulbs and two switches, make the bulbs turn on and off independently.

- Using two batteries, two bulbs and two switches, make the bulbs turn on and off independently, but make it so that closing the switches turns the bulbs OFF.

- Use two, more complex, switches to make a staircase light than can be turned on or off from both switches (one at the bottom of the stairs, one at the top).

So, by the beginning of this next lesson, the class were *au fait* with 'Crocodile Clips' and I was ready to move them on to the next sub-topic, 'Measuring Current'. The work from the first lesson did not really require 'Crocodile Clips', although there are some advantages in using it here even so; the understanding of how a 'real' circuit works often fails to transfer to 'symbolic' circuits, but because 'Crocodile Clips' builds working symbolic circuits, this connection is that much stronger (and after all, symbolic circuits are the ones that the students will have to handle in their SATs exams next year). Also the two-dimensionality of the computer screen and the method 'Crocodile Clips' uses to link components (straight lines and square corners) means that under-standing is not obfuscated by the typical 'spaghetti junction' look of the circuits built in practical lessons.

The other development at the end of the first lesson, as confidence with the program increased and concentration waned, was the beginning of 'free experimentation' with the components and menus of the program. This was also the first thing that began happening when I asked them to log in at the beginning of the second lesson, as screens quickly became filled with 'crazy' circuits during the taking of the register.

Then came a nexus point – the class really seemed to be enjoying using the program in this way, finding a sort of liberation in the unlim-itedness of the components available, in sharp contrast to the shortages they had experienced in the previous practical lessons. Also, at the back of my mind when I planned this lesson, there was the advantage that, especially when trying to understand the behaviour of current in circuits, the opportunity to use multiple ammeters is a huge advantage.

In class, with a full set of ammeters being twelve, this is only possible in demonstration. The other option is a laborious and often quite confusing movement of the ammeter around the circuit into different positions (with no guarantee of the same readings – the change of even the last figure in digital display often destroys the impression of 'sameness'). 'Crocodile Clips' gives an exciting alternative.

For me, the real challenge here was having the courage to 'go with the flow' and channel something that was happening already through self-motivation into fulfilling my learning objectives for the lesson (and trusting I could think on my feet fast enough to stay one step ahead of the class and take in all the original 'bases'). So rather than 'shutting down' what was already going on and hauling the class back to my original lesson plan, I called to class to focus and said that they could make a circuit, as big as they liked, but only using batteries, bulbs and ammeters with a 'connection' rule of 'no branches or junctions'. The entire class laid into this with gusto and I soon had screens brim full with the components.

Back to focus, we talked briefly about what they noticed about the numbers on the ammeters (they had no idea at this point what an ammeter was or what the numbers meant).

'Okay, remove some bulbs. What happens to the numbers'.

'What about the brightness of the remaining bulbs?'

'What happens if you put in more batteries? What do you think might happen to the numbers? ... Try it. See if you're right.'

'What do you think those numbers might tell us then?'

'Put a bulb and an ammeter in parallel with another bulb and ammeter.'

'What happened? ... What is the connection between the numbers on those two ammeters and all the rest?'

'Try that somewhere else.'

'Did the same thing happen?'

'What do you think might happen if you put three bulb and ammeter sets in parallel?' ... Okay, try it.'

I was then able to seamlessly rejoin the original teaching plan for the lesson, having established 'the rules for the behaviour of current in circuits' in a way the students had enjoyed and found accessible, I had simply not imagined before and was impossible to do physically in any realistic sense. And I think this is the real power if ICT; it is a tool for providing learning experiences previously impossible, previously impractical or simply previously beyond our imagination.

A process model of learning

A means of looking more closely at the role of ICT as scaffolding is provided by a process model of learning (Kolb 1984, Denison and Kirk 1990), consisting of a repeating cycle (shown below in Figure 2). Students carry out (*do*) a range of activities to introduce new skills and concepts. They reflect upon and discuss (*review*) their action in order to internalise and make sense of (*learn*) what they have done. They will utilise (*apply*) what they have learned in developing their work and also in future learning contexts.

In carrying out any given task, a student may work his/her way around this cycle many times, rethinking ideas, discussing possibilities, receiving advice and improving outcomes. In describing the stages of this learning cycle Kolb stresses the shift from a 'concrete experience', where feelings play an important part, to 'abstract conceptualisation', where thinking is more important. It is 'reflective observation' that helps students to understand their experiences, bringing about the shift from concrete to abstract. The resulting 'active experimentation' leads to the testing of new ideas and improvements to what has already been done.

Honey and Mumford (1992) have added to this model by describing the learning styles at each stage. At the *do* stage the learner is an 'activist', getting involved in the experience and rising to the challenge. At the *review* stage the learner is a 'reflector', carefully observing and considering what has been done before reaching any conclusions. At the *learn* stage the learner is a 'theorist', developing sensible theories after systematic analysis of the problem at hand. At the *apply* stage the learner is a 'pragmatist', getting on with the practical job of implementing solutions. Individual students are likely to fall naturally into one of these four roles over and above the others. But by structuring learning towards this process model, teachers can make students aware of their predominant learning style and help them move beyond their usual roles. As Watkins et al (1998, p. 3) have pointed out, students 'learn more effectively...when they have learned about their own learning'. There are many ways in which ICT can support each stage of the do-review-learn-apply cycle, as shown in Figure 2 and described in more detail below.

Figure 2 ICT as a tool for active learning – the learning cycle

▬ Stages of the *do – review – learn – apply* cycle

▬ The *do* stage

In the *do* stage of the learning cycle, ICT can be a vehicle for active independent or collaborative work, where students are engaged in activities organised or set by the teacher. ICT allows students to experiment with ideas. General-purpose software, such as word processors, graphics packages and data-handling tools, allow ideas to be entered, edited and shaped easily. In this respect it is important that ICT is not simply seen as a means of 'typing-up work in best'. Used effectively it allows students to actually develop their work and thoughts directly into the machine, and as such offers them the ultimate thinking tool. The vast quantities of information now available through ICT media, particularly CD-ROMs and the Internet, enable students to gather material from a range of sources for use within their work. ICT might also be used to facilitate basic tasks, such as text layout, graph plotting, music production and so on. In getting basic tasks done quickly and efficiently, students and teachers have more time at their disposal for higher-order activities such as interpreting, hypothesising and modelling. ICT can put the student in a situation where exploration and prediction can take place and instant outcomes of the decisions taken can be seen. For example, simulations in which the user has to adopt a particular role can lead to valuable discussion, decision-making and action. Similarly, more open-ended modelling environments, such as LOGO or spreadsheets, enable the design and exploration of simulated reality. In all these active uses of ICT the student is in a position where trial and error is possible. Mistakes can be made and corrected easily, ideas can be trialled and accepted or rejected, hypotheses can be formed and tested.

The *review* stage

The *review* stage of the cycle may be reached automatically, as the student reaches a point in their work where some reflection is required, or it could be prompted by peer or teacher intervention. It is the crucial point in the use of ICT where particular ideas that have been developed in the activity are compared with other ideas that the student has. These ideas may also be shared with others involved in the learning process – friends, teachers, parents et alia. The review stage might also involve the careful consideration of information that has been gathered, checking for relevance and validity, and rejecting information that is not useful. This is particularly important when using ICT-based resources such as the Internet, where much of the information is of unknown or dubious origin. Students need to learn how to search for information they need, sift through it, acknowledge what is helpful, synthesise it with other ideas and information, and discard the rest. Basic tasks that have been accomplished quickly through using ICT allow more time for key questions to be posed:

- Why did that happen?
- What does this mean/show?
- How can I describe this?
- What conclusions can be drawn?
- How can I improve this work?

Results that have been arrived at through exploration and prediction can be analysed and interpreted in order to look for significant patterns or relationships. Most importantly, the review stage in the learning process allows students the opportunity to look for improvements in their work with assistance from others, identifying gaps in their understanding as a result of trial and error.

■■■■ The *learn* stage

The *learn* stage of the learning cycle is perhaps the most difficult to describe because it involves some sort of internalisation of meaning from the previous stages. It is hard to specify exactly what is internalised from any given activity, but some of the main indicators that learning has taken place can be suggested. Having experimented with ideas and then compared and shared them with others, a student might be expected to develop new ideas which build on the originals. When information has been gathered and sifted, some of it will be absorbed, if only temporarily, so that it can be used and applied in later tasks with an appreciation of its meaning. Another manifestation of learning might be the formulation of answers to key questions that have been raised as a result of practical work. For example, a graph produced quickly using ICT might have led to the question: 'Why is there an upward trend?' The student could then combine this new evidence with what they already know in order to find an explanation. The outcome of analysis and interpretation of results collected from an exploratory activity might be to reach some conclusions or generalisations about what the results mean. And, having identified improvements to a particular piece of work after a process of trial and error, judgements can be made as to what constitutes a 'better' outcome.

■■■■ The *apply* stage

The *apply* stage of the process model might involve the use of what has been learned within the same task, or a different task. The transfer of knowledge and skills between tasks is not always straightforward, particularly across subjects in a secondary school, and perhaps ICT can facilitate this transfer. For example, new ideas that have arisen from experimentation and review can be employed using ICT to edit, store and retrieve. Similarly, information that has been collected, sifted and stored for one task can easily be retrieved for reusing within another. Another way in which ICT can assist movement around the learning cycle comes from the quick implementation of basic tasks. Because time is made available for higher-order thinking and questioning, more complex tasks can be attempted in following up answers. When using ICT as a tool for exploration and prediction, interpretations and conclusions that are drawn can lead to further exploration and prediction. Finally, and most importantly, when applying what they have learned students are able to implement improvements to their work, demonstrating higher levels of skill and better understanding.

Taking advantage of ICT

In order to take full advantage of ICT at every stage of the learning cycle, easy access to resources both during and outside of lesson times is required. Increasingly students have ICT facilities available in the home – the McKinsey Report (1997) states that in 1997, 22% of UK households owned fairly modern computers, and extrapolates an increase to 45–55% by 2001. A survey carried out in 1998 indicated that 66% of Hampstead School students had a modern computer at home. However, there will always be some students who do not have access to ICT at home and those who do may not always have the range of resources that schools can offer. The following case study highlights some of the benefits and challenges involved in providing open ICT access for students.

 Case Study 10 – Independent Learning Centre

In the school library (or Independent Learning Centre, as it is known), ICT is most commonly used by students doing homework, particularly for set tasks. This often involves research using the Internet or networked CD-ROMs. The school provides an 'Internet Gateway' page, which contains a list of subject-related links to direct students towards websites we want them to use. Students also use search engines to find more specific information. Many students use the various ICT tools (such as Word, Excel, Powerpoint and Publisher) to do their work, building on ICT skills they have learned within the curriculum. Some students use the library as a 'printing service', bringing in work they have done at home on disk for printing. They particularly like printing their work in colour.

There are clear benefits to students' learning in providing open access to ICT facilities. On the research side, there seems to be less of a barrier for students in finding what they want from a computer compared with the use of books. I don't know exactly why this is, but it has a lot to do with the motivation of ICT. Access to ICT has certainly meant that a wider range of students uses the library more often. This creates a more inclusive environment in which we can promote a greater interest in books as well as ICT. When using ICT the students also seem to take more pride in their work, particularly if they struggle with handwriting. They can produce work which is generally neat and well-presented, they can delete their mistakes without others seeing, and tools such as Powerpoint help them to prepare better presentations. Other literacy skills are supported by ICT as it allows them to think in a different way. Students see ICT as a non-threatening tool, approaching the machines with a confidence they do not always have with other people. ICT often leads to independence, although students also help each other with what they are doing.

There have been several challenges involved in making ICT openly available in the Independent Learning Centre. Students often produce work that looks neat, but which they have not checked carefully for mistakes. They frequently forget to spell-check their work, ignoring the automatic underlining of miss-spelt words. There is also a tendency for students to print out large amounts of information from CD-ROMs or the Internet without reading it for understanding. This is not a new problem as students used to photocopy large chunks of books, but ICT has made it easier for them. We are trying hard to educate students to be more selective with information, comparing different sources with their own ideas, and also to think about content before presentation.

Many students just want to 'surf' the Internet, with no real aim in mind. There is nothing wrong with this, but the surfers sometimes prevent others from working. So a job for us is to make sure that those who want to work can. Another challenge for us is in deciding where to draw the line between acceptable and unacceptable material. Our Internet Code (see Appendix 2) prohibits access to material that is racist, sexist or obscene, so pornography is definitely banned, but what about the ever-popular wrestling pictures? As well as using an Internet service provider that filters out inappropriate sites we also have our own blocking system, but new sites appear on the Web every day and students have a way of finding them. Sometimes what first appears to be unacceptable use of the Internet can prove to be innocent and work-related. Some students who were recently found looking at semi-naked bodies were actually researching body piercing and tattooing as part of a DT project. Similarly, do we allow students to access games on the Internet? We generally do not make games available on our networks, but what about educational ones like chess? Deciding where to draw these lines is a major challenge. The answer to most of these problems is clear, simple guidelines combined with careful supervision.

■ Conclusion

For models of learning (like those considered above) to be useful in practice, staff and students need to be aware of them and relate them to their own learning. Such an awareness 'gives people the key to the learning process and allows them to unlock their full potential' (Lockitt, 1997, p. 18). Used effectively, ICT can contribute to learning – providing 'scaffolding' at each stage, thereby 'driving' the learner around the cycle as a whole. In this way ICT helps 'reinforce the notion that learning itself is interactive' (Birnbaum, 1990, p. 15), enabling students to move beyond any predominant learning styles and, perhaps, to increase their self-awareness. To summarise the role of ICT as a tool for active learning:

■ Ideas can be entered, organised and edited easily, leading to the development and employment of new ideas, perhaps after some collaboration with others.

■ Large amounts of information from a range of sources can be searched for, gathered, checked and sifted, then used or transferred to other tasks.

■ Tasks that would be slow to accomplish manually can be done quickly, allowing time for questions to be posed and answered, and more complex tasks to be tackled.

■ Exploration and prediction can lead to instant feedback, so that situations can be analysed and interpreted easily, and conclusions can be drawn.

■ A learning environment is provided in which ideas and information can be changed through a process of trial and error, and improvements can be made easily.

Main points

■ Learning with ICT is a very active process.

■ ICT can motivate learning.

■ Teaching can be viewed as 'assisted performance'.

■ The learning process can be viewed as a repeating cycle in four stages: do – review – learn – apply.

■ ICT can assist learning: 'scaffolding' each stage of the learning cycle and 'driving' the learner around it.

5 Learning environments and types of software

'The computer is the Proteus of machines. Its essence is its universality, its power to simulate. Because it can take on a thousand forms and can serve a thousand functions, it can appeal to a thousand tastes.'

(Papert, 1980, p. viii)

One of the most exciting aspects of ICT in schools is the virtually limit-less applicability of the technology itself. The computer is perhaps the ultimate tool: it allows the collection, processing, presentation and communication of information on any subject. It can model almost any situation, allowing us to simulate and analyse real-life events; it provides the underlying controlling structures for much of the other technology that shapes the modern world; it can provide new ways for people to work, both independently and collaboratively. The flex-ibility of ICT may also allow us to 'tap in' to more of our students' intelligences. Gardner (1993) has identified eight types of intelligence:

- linguistic;
- mathematical;
- musical;
- visual;
- physical;
- interpersonal;
- intrapersonal;
- naturalistic.

Most of these can be developed with the assistance of ICT, which offers huge scope for the creation of different learning environments. The technological contribution to the working or learning environment is largely provided by the software, which shapes the interaction between the user or student and the machine. However, the use of ICT does not in any way imply a reduced role for the teacher. The particular set of teaching and learning objectives that he/she defines will determine the precise nature of the learning environment. As Pachler (1999, p. 7) points out, the teacher's role 'remains pivotal, such as in identifying appropriate learning outcomes, choosing appropriate software and activities, and structuring and sequencing the learning process'. In this chapter the main types of software that can be found in schools are described and classified, before looking more closely at the learning environments they support.

▓ Generic and specific software

The skills and activities that make up ICT capability within the national curriculum are most commonly taught via the use of generic, or general-purpose software, such as word processors, graphics programs, databases, spreadsheets and so on. Generic programs have little or no subject matter or content contained within them – they are content-free. They are essentially tools for carrying out and facilitating tasks, like text production and data handling. Such programs are often described as emancipatory, as they can free the user from otherwise tedious and time-consuming work, leaving time for development of ideas and higher-order tasks. As Bruner (1996, p. 2) suggests, 'a well-programmed computer is especially useful for taking over tasks that, at last, can be declared "unfit for human production" '. Generic software programs, despite being content-free, usually impose certain parameters on the user in the range of features they provide and the mode of operation they demand. In addition, schools often make use of specific software, recent forms of which include reference tools (such as CD-ROMs) and integrated learning systems (ILS). This type of software differs from generic software, in that it is content carrying. With generic software it is the user who generates the content; with specific software the content is built into its design. Some types of specific software attempt to teach concepts or skills by presenting them in various ways and involving students in activities. This use of ICT is often referred to as computer assisted learning (CAL) or computer assisted instruction (CAI).

Though there are relationships between generic and specific software, it is possible to combine the use of each type, for example, by finding useful information from a CD-ROM and then reworking it for a presentation using a desktop publishing or graphics program. Other situations where generic software can be used for specific purposes are when a computer model of a situation is set up using a spreadsheet. The teacher creates the model using a generic program, but for the students the content is already defined. Similarly, a wordprocessor can be used to present text to students for reworking. This can help to overcome the 'blank sheet' problem (see Case study 15 – Music in chapter 6) where the creative potential of content-free software is too daunting. Structured activities with some teacher-provided content can lead to more open-ended creative work.

Different types of generic and specific software currently available are outlined in the table below. Some programs fall into more than one category.

GENERIC SOFTWARE – general purpose, productivity tools, content free

Word processing and DTP	For producing documents, essays, reports, presentations
Graphics packages	For painting, drawing, illustrating, designing, presenting
Databases and spreadsheets	For handling data, charting, modelling analysing, predicting
Modelling tools	For creating models of situations or processes
Authoring programs	For creating multimedia presentations and applications
Programming languages	For creating computer applications
Measurement and control programs	For collecting data from sensors and controlling external devices
Internet communication tools	For browsing, e-mail, file transfer, conferencing
Other tools	For making music, accounting, organisers, etc.

SPECIFIC SOFTWARE – subject related, computer assisted learning, content carrying

Drill and practice programs	For question and answer, trial and error, challenges, text manipulation andreconstructtion, simple games
Closed simulations	For simulating situations or processes, learner makes decisions (changes variables) which alter the outcome, 'closed' – limited outcomes
Open simulations	For exploring situations or processes, learner can control 'rules' of the situation, 'open' – unlimited outcomes, 'Microworlds'
Integrated learning systems (ILS)	Complete systems, wide range of skills and concepts taught, mainly 'instructional' but becoming more interactive, diagnostic, individualised to pupil's needs, can produce reports of pupil progress
Information sources (CD-ROMs, large databases, World Wide Web)	Resources for browsing and extracting information, often multimedia – text, pictures, sounds, animations and video

▮ Learning environments

One of the greatest benefits afforded by such a wide range of available software is the variety of different *learning environments* that can be supported. The type of software and the way in which it is used greatly affect the learning environment in which the user is placed. There are opportunities for many different activities, such as:

- private study;
- group work;
- problem solving and decision making;
- role play;
- tests and challenges;
- investigative work and fact finding.

The following case study describes the range of software used in Design and Technology at Hampstead School and the different types of learning promoted.

▮ Case study 11 – Design and Technology

ICT is used in Design and Technology (D&T) for graphic applications, control and CAD/CAM. The students gradually develop good graphical presentation skills and learn that the end product in any project can be the result of more than one application. They become used to creating graphics in one program and using them within another, so that a project involves the integration of a number of applications. In this way, students learn the differences between applications and develop knowledge of the appropriate software for particular jobs. Students frequently explore this on their own. For one project (designing a chocolate bar wrapper), the students start with a template in CorelDraw. Some students stay within CorelDraw from start to finish, using the various features of the software to complete the job. Others use more familiar programs (such as the WordArt feature in Microsoft Word) to produce parts of the design and then copy and paste them back into CorelDraw. In D&T, ICT allows students to be relatively autonomous in what they do. Some students are very independent and have the confidence to experiment and get things wrong. Different versions of a piece of work, showing various designs and colour schemes, can be produced quickly without labouring over them.

For the initial teaching of control, simple and easy-to-use software is important. It is hard enough for the students to understand the terminology (input, output, process etc.), and in Year 7 a big part of the traffic light project is understanding which commands are used for which action. The software we use (Logicator) is very pictorial, based on a flowchart diagram, which helps students to make a visual and mental link with the concepts without using a complex programming language. The physical equipment (lights, switches etc.) helps them to see how the information is processed, where it comes from and where it goes to, reinforcing the key ideas. This provides a hands-on experience that students find motivating. The results are so immediate – they can see an instant response to what they've done. As a minimum, all students manage to make the lights work to the correct sequence. The majority also understand how to control an input, i.e. a switch that activates a pelican crossing. This is represented in the flowchart by the question 'Is the switch pressed?' and, depending on the answer, the course of the flowchart is diverted to stop the traffic. Students can extend this work by making the system more realistic – adding sound when the pedestrians cross, adding flashing amber lights and correct timings etc. The students can make these improvements through trial and error experimentation. The work students do in designing control systems helps them to understand CAD/CAM and other more advanced control systems that they use later on.

One of the main challenges of using ICT in D&T is getting round to help everybody when one-to-one assistance is needed. However, this problem is decreasing as students come into the school with better skills. The interactive whiteboard is extremely useful for demonstrating skills to a whole class at once. In control lessons, it is a great feat to get all the equipment set up and put away. You can start the lesson in a 'flap' having spent 20 minutes beforehand setting everything up. If the students are expected to set up and put away there is often insufficient time to cover the lesson. Classroom assistance makes a huge difference – the assistant can be setting up while you introduce the lesson – and the students also get better support. The wide range of software available is another challenge. Staff can feel that they 'just can't cope with all of this'. The solution is partly provided through in-class and out-of-class support from ICT specialists. Staff development is ongoing – little chunks of information and help gradually build expertise that can be shared among the department. Most importantly, staff need to ask one another for help.

■ From instruction, through construction to co-construction

In looking more closely at learning environments, it is useful to identify three main types of learning:

■ instruction;

■ construction;

■ co-construction.

Figure 3 summarises the main types of software used in schools and broadly indicates the learning environments that are supported by each.

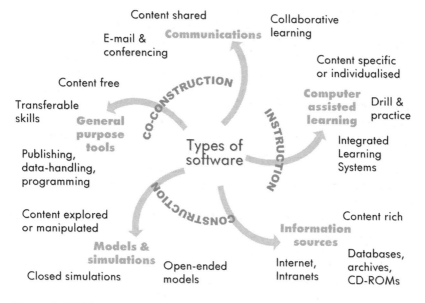

Figure 3 ICT learning environments – types of software

Instruction involves learning by being shown or told, drawing upon behaviourist theories of conditioning and reinforcement. Many of the specific software types described above fit into this category, particularly drill and practice programs and integrated learning systems. These focus on the delivery of subject content in small 'chunks', repetitive skills practice and positive reinforcement of correct responses. *Construction* involves learning by building meaning from active experiences, rooted in cognitive theories of information processing and constructivism. Generic software packages clearly lend themselves to this type of learning, whereby information and ideas can be collected, developed and processed in order to build understanding. Models and simulations, both generic and subject specific, also provide opportunities for constructing knowledge through exploration and problem-solving. Papert's ideas for the use of the programming language LOGO (mentioned in chapter 4) clearly exemplify this type of learning. *Co-construction* involves learning within and as part of a community of learners, taking into account socio-cultural theories of communication and interaction with others. Watkins (2000) explains: 'Learning is fostered through co-construction, exchanging narratives in the process we call dialogue'. While ICT is likely to have an increasing role in mediating this interaction as Internet-based on-line learning communities become more prevalent, it is the teacher's organisation of the learning environment that is crucial. To encourage co-construction when using the Internet, or any other form of ICT, the teacher should enable 'pupils to work together with peers in pairs or groups and engage in discussions and reflection' (Pachler, 1999, p. 59). So the contribution of ICT to learning environments based on co-construction has less to do with the software itself than the context the teacher creates for its use.

Generic and specific software can both be used to promote collaborative work by careful setting of tasks and grouping of students. As Schofield (1995, p. 228) has explained, computers 'are social as well as technological objects, and their use is subject to the vagaries of the social milieu in which they are available for use, although over time they may profoundly influence that milieu'. One account of how ICT has been used to facilitate co-constructivist learning is provided in the case study below.

■ Case study 12 – Science

The use of ICT within Science is a requirement of the National Curriculum, which states 'pupils should be given opportunities to choose ways of using IT to collect, store, retrieve and present scientific information'. It is now therefore not a case of 'should we use datalogging equipment?', but 'how should we use it in order to maximise the benefits to our students?' I believe that the most effective way that we can teach science or scientific inquiry is to employ constructivist ideals. One of the key ideas of social constructivism is that discussion enables students to explore, test and affirm their ideas and that group development of these ideas is greater than that of the individual. Practical work in groups therefore provides frequent opportunity for student discussion and the subsequent development of their scientific understanding.

The 'scientific investigation' chapter of the National Curriculum provides an excellent opportunity for the effective use of data-logging, which can be categorised into five distinct approaches:

1. *Demonstration* – There are many reasons why demonstrations are used in the science classroom, the most obvious being that equipment is limited or the practical is too dangerous for the students to do themselves. However, there is also a possibility that the equipment being used is too valuable or fragile for the students to use and, unfortunately, computers and data-logging equipment are often seen in this light. As a result the students do not get to use them.

2. *Large groups* – Large groups are generally used when equipment is scarce. Students could benefit from a wider range of contributions to discussion, however, it is often the case in large group situations that some students will either be unwilling to discuss their ideas or they will not be able to due to other more dominant members.

3. *One-to-one in class and as an extension activity* – In the first of these situations all students have a data-logger and perform the experiment by themselves. Although the student may benefit from more hands-on experience of the equipment, from a social constructivist standpoint student learning will be limited if they are not encouraged to discuss the results with their peers. The second of these situations enables the more able to use data-logging equipment as an extension activity. I would argue that it is the less able that gain maximum benefit from data-logging activities as it enables them to explore and develop their ideas without the fear of falling behind with graph plotting or recording of results.

4. *One small group and the rest of the class with traditional equipment* – This enables some students (for example, the less able) to benefit from the advantages that the equipment can provide, and enables others to see the benefits. This is again the type of situation that occurs if the equipment is limited.

5. *Small groups* – I would argue that this is the optimum situation as it enables all members of a group to develop the skills needed to use data-logging equipment but also facilitates group discussion in which all group members can participate.

I feel that data-logging can successfully enhance Science taught from a variety of perspectives as it enables all students to access a large amount of accurate data in an easy to comprehend graphical format that relates to the events in front of them. The teacher's approach will determine how data-logging is used and the extent of the benefit to student learning. I would argue that the greatest advantages of data-logging are the time saved during an experiment leading to discussion of the data, and the graphical representations of the results facilitating a greater understanding of the data. This additional time provides an opportunity for small group discussions, which can yield great advances in the students' thinking as they explore each others' ideas.

Advantages of ILS

Specific software based upon instruction through individualised drill and practice will offer little scope for social interaction, and serious concerns have been expressed that such programs 'may cause more harm than good if used too soon and too extensively' (Healy, 1999, p. 234). Nevertheless, in recent years, integrated learning systems (ILS) have been shown to help bring about impressive learning gains in numeracy and literacy (Wood, 1998). Therefore, if instructional software is to be used it should be as just one component of a much broader range of teaching and learning strategies. At Hampstead School, like many others, an ILS is used with half a class for half the lesson while the remainder of the group has an intensive interactive session with the teacher. Halfway through the lesson the two groups swap over so that all students experience both a very individualised, computer-based instructional approach preceded or followed by a small group-focused, teacher-led session looking at similar work. The following case study describes the use of integrated learning systems in Maths, as well as some more constructivist approaches to ICT in Maths lessons.

Case study 13 – Maths

In Maths (and also in English) we use SuccessMaker, an integrated learning system, focusing on 11- to 14-year-olds. It gives questions on a variety of Maths topics, pitched at the appropriate level for students to achieve 70% to 80% success. It's almost like a teacher – if a student gets something wrong it re-phrases the question or 'steps back' to give them easier questions, boosting their confidence and helping them to move on. The program can pinpoint a particular problem in any child's understanding of Maths, so that the teacher can intervene at that stage.

It's quite interactive too. Students have their virtual Maths equipment on screen (rulers, protractors, calculators etc.) available to use. As well as improving numeracy they are learning to use this type of equipment. The mental arithmetic speed games are a favourite feature, where students have to answer questions as quickly as possible and they want to beat their previous score. A lot of praise is built into the program and students can display their score cards. National Curriculum levels for every topic can be identified easily and homework sheets can be printed for each student at the right level. The homework sheets double-up as a record of the level that each student is working to, as they contain similar questions to those done on the computer. Later, in Years 9 and 10, students start to use the Headstart ILS, which is designed like a traditional GCSE course with a syllabus, tutorials, a practice area (lab) and tests. Teachers can set up work plans for students to carry out, covering the desired material, and then monitor individual progress. It has a large bank of GCSE questions to help students prepare for exams.

The huge benefit of both SuccessMaker and Headstart is the fact they are differentiated. Each child gets work that is appropriate for them. Students are motivated because they are not trying to do too many things that they find difficult. With half the class using these programs at a time, as a teacher you can focus on the rest of the group to give them 'quality time'. This is because integrated learning systems allow students to work independently. Students have a Maths resource that can tell them how to do it, practise it and then test it. From a teacher's point of view, the fact that Headstart can write a test for you in about two minutes on any chosen Maths topic, and then administer it, mark it and give feedback on the students' performance is extremely useful.

For SuccessMaker to realise learning gains it has to be used constantly, and time allocation has proved difficult due to timetabling constraints. Another problem is that the techniques taught within the program do not always link in with the National Numeracy Strategy. For example, with vertical subtraction SuccessMaker does not allow carrying into the next column. Also, students have to type in answers from left to right, but on paper they would normally be entered from right to left across the columns (units, tens, hundreds, etc.). So students end up using methods different from those they have been taught elsewhere. One solution is to remove these types of question from within the SuccessMaker management system, which is extremely flexible.

As well as integrated learning systems, students experience a wide range of more creative uses of ICT within the Maths curriculum, including data handling, graph plotting, transformations, spreadsheet modelling and LOGO. With LOGO they start with basic commands to draw shapes. They can draw very quickly, having the opportunity to make mistakes, rethink and start again. They build on their LOGO skill while simultaneously learning Maths concepts, writing procedures to explore interior and exterior angles in polygons. When programming in this way they make the connection between exterior angle and number of sides much quicker than they would using pen and paper. LOGO encourages students to be investigative – they can use trial and error/improvement to look for patterns and rules. This can lead to the design of procedures that use variables.

■ The balance of control

One way to examine more closely the learning environments a particular computer program can support is to look at the *balance of control* between the computer and the user. Different ICT applications offer the user different levels of control and each user will have his or her own perception of, and way of dealing with, this control. At one extreme the computer is completely in control, for example – a demonstration program. At the other extreme the user is in total control of the computer, for example – when programming. Most applications lie somewhere between these two extremes and identifying the balance of control is useful when evaluating their potential for learning. A continuum can be used to represent the balance of control between the computer and the user, as shown in Figure 4. Characteristics of the computer ▦ and the user ☺ are described at four stages along the continuum, and examples of ICT activities are given. (Note: The locations of the ICT activities given are approximate.)

The balance of control between the computer and the user will vary according to the design of the ICT application itself, the context in which it is being used, and the characteristics of the user. Taking these features one at a time, some applications are designed to promote several different activities and could therefore occupy more than one position on the continuum. For example, a simulation program may include demonstrations and also investigations. Similarly, reference tools can be used for general browsing, more structured inquiries, or extracts may be taken for inclusion in a presentation. The context in which an application is being used will also affect the balance of control. For example, a graphics program can be used in a completely open-ended way, as a tool for creative expression. Alternatively, the teacher could use the same program to give the students a particular design or pattern to edit, perhaps by trying out different colour-

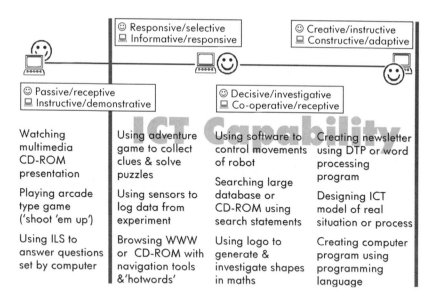

Figure 4 ICT learning environments – balance of control

schemes. The experience and characteristics of the user may also be significant. A positive approach to the application, together with guidance from a teacher, can lead to shifts along the continuum towards more user-controlled activities.

▮▮ Conclusion

ICT, due to its inherent versatility, can help to promote a wide variety of learning environments, the nature of which are strongly influenced by the balance of control between the computer and the user. This can be represented as a continuum of learning environments, ranging from instructive to constructive. The potential of ICT for supporting collaborative work, combined with skilful teaching, can create co-constructive learning environments. The balance of control continuum also helps to define ICT capability, which demands a certain level of control by the user (as indicated in Figure 4). The further to the right along the continuum an activity is placed, the software used tends to be more generic, the learning environment more constructive, and the user is increasingly in 'the driving seat' – students do not acquire ICT capability just by sitting at a computer. This does not imply that activities on the far left of the continuum are worthless.

Specific software such as integrated learning systems (ILS) and drill and practice programs, while allowing the learner little or no control over the computer, can provide valuable learning opportunities when used in an appropriate context. An important message here is that not all ICT-based activities contribute to the acquisition of ICT capability. Many activities, for example using an information source (perhaps a CD-ROM) to carry out some historical research, clearly involve elements of ICT capability. Others, such as computer-based question and answer exercises, however valuable as a learning aid, do not. In chapter 6 of this book the skills that comprise ICT capability are examined more closely.

▉▉▉ Main points

■ ICT is a very flexible and adaptable tool.

■ ICT can create a wide range of learning environments.

■ Software is either 'generic' or 'specific' in nature.

■ The teacher has a vital role in defining ICT-based learning environments.

■ ICT capability involves a degree of control over the computer by the user.

6 What is ICT capability?

'If you can use a computer, then it will help you learn, write, design, make graphs and much, much more.'   (Year 7 student, 2000)

Using ICT as a tool for learning means that students must 'get their hands dirty' with the technology. Teaching how ICT *can* be used is not enough. It is vital that students are given opportunities to try things for themselves. This imperative for hands-on experience is exemplified by the term *ICT capability* within the National Curriculum. Knowledge of when and how to use ICT effectively is also a part of being 'ICT capable'. This chapter addresses the question 'what is ICT capability?'

IT becomes ICT

The term *IT capability* was introduced with the National Curriculum in 1989, ten years before the 'C' in ICT was added. The word 'capability' is a fitting reminder that the range of skills involved in using ICT as an effective tool for learning are 'concerned with practical action' (NCC, 1990). ICT – information and **communication** technology – has now largely replaced IT in educational terminology, but has not been adopted by business and industry. The terms IT and ICT are synonymous, despite the fact that some interesting, but largely irrelevant distinctions have been attempted and rejected. (For a while the notion was peddled that *IT* was a set of skills and *ICT* was the equipment with which those skills were exercised.)

The 1997 report commissioned by Tony Blair and David Blunkett (independently of the Labour Party) under the chairmanship of Dennis Stephenson seems to be the first use of the term ICT in the UK, emphasising the importance of communications technologies, particularly the Internet. Since then, it has been used in the National Grid for Learning initiative and in the National Curriculum orders for September 2000. The leading suppliers of educational technology have readily adopted the term and the rest of the educational world has followed. This change of terminology is significant. Not only does it express the current educational interest in the use of the Internet, intranets and video conferencing, it has been used by central government to repackage, take ownership and raise the status of technological initiatives in schools. The revised National Curriculum for 2000 states that:

> *'Information and communication technology (ICT) prepares pupils to participate in a rapidly changing world in which work and other activities are increasingly transformed by access to varied and developing technology. Pupils use ICT tools to find, explore, analyse, exchange and present information responsibly, creatively and with discrimination. They learn how to employ ICT to enable rapid access to ideas and experiences from a wide range of people, communities and cultures. Increased capability in the use of ICT promotes initiative and independent learning, with pupils being able to make informed judgements about when and where to use ICT to best effect, and to consider its implications for home and work both now and in the future.'*
>
> (DfEE/QCA, 1999, p. 14.)

Strands of capability

The non-statutory guidance that accompanied the original National Curriculum divided 'IT' capability (as it was then known) into five strands (see table below).

Original strands of capability

Communicating information	Communicating ideas in different contexts, taking audiences into account. Integrating and presenting different forms of information, such as text, graphics, sounds, animation and video, as appropriate.
Handling information	Storage, processing and analysis of qualitative and quantitative information. Using different information sources to select and display information, questioning its plausibility.
Modelling	Using models and simulations to explore real and imaginary situations, predicting outcomes and identifying patterns and relationships. Designing and creating computer-based models.
Measurement and control	Collecting various types of physical data using sensors and the computerised control of devices and events.
Applications and effects	Reviewing IT experiences, examining the advantages and disadvantages, relating them to wider applications. Discussion of the social, economic and moral issues relating to IT.

The five strands of IT capability consisted of four broad application groups (communicating information, handling information, modelling and measurement and control) plus one general strand (applications and effects) involving the review of practical work and wider issues. This breaking down of the IT requirements was useful as it provided a framework for understanding and organising the skills involved. It also helped in identifying subject areas that might provide opportunities for the development and application of IT capability, for example, measurement and control activities find their natural place in the Science, Maths and Design & Technology curricula. In the revised National Curriculum for 2000 (DfEE/QCA, 1999). ICT capability is presented in four new strands (see table below).

At first sight the new strands appear to be a simple renaming of the old ones.

- 'Finding things out' corresponds to 'handling information'.

- 'Developing ideas and making things happen' roughly map to 'modelling' and 'measurement and control' respectively.

- 'Exchanging and sharing information' is an extension of 'communicating information'.

- 'Reviewing, modifying and evaluating work...' is comparable with 'applications and effects'.

Furthermore, the actual skills that comprise ICT capability remain much as before, with the specific addition of e-mail as a means of sharing and exchanging information. However, the new strands represent a more fundamental shift of emphasis. Where the old strands

Revised strands of capability

Finding things out	Gathering, selecting, preparing and processing information in a variety of forms and from a range of sources. Interrogating information sources carefully and using information discriminately.
Developing ideas and making things happen	Exploring and developing information and models, in order to solve problems and to identify patterns and relationships. Measuring, recording and controlling events.
Exchanging and sharing information	Organising and presenting different forms of information for a range of purposes and audiences. Sharing and exchanging information electronically.
Reviewing, modifying and evaluating work as it progresses	Reflecting on practice in order to improve work and to judge the effectiveness of ICT. Discussing the wider impact of ICT on individuals, communities and society.

delineate groups of *applications*, the new strands focus on the *processes* involved.

The change of focus reflects the blurring of distinctions between computer applications as they have evolved in recent years. For example, data-handling applications often have well-developed presentation and reporting tools; likewise publishing software sometimes has built-in data-handling tools. The particular application used for any given purpose has become less important than the process involved in the task. The change of language used in the new strands also appears to be a conscious effort to use non-technical terms, designed to be more accessible to students, parents and subject teachers. The order in which the strands are presented is also significant, reflecting a cycle of information skills:

- collecting and preparing;

- exploring and developing;

- organising and presenting;

- exchanging and sharing;

- reviewing, evaluating and improving.

This sequencing of skills closely resembles the process model of learning (do – review – learn – apply cycle) considered in Chapter 4. Figure 5 shows the relationship between the old and new strands – the cycle of processes can be exercised using a wide range of ICT applications in a variety of subject contexts.

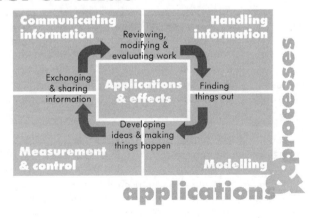

Figure 5 ICT capability – old and new strands

Case study 14 illustrates the importance of processes as well as products, describing how Art students use ICT both to create finished pieces and to develop ideas.

■ Case study 14 – Art

In one particular project, A-level students had to explore the way they feel about their own bodies. First they drew around each other using a large sheet of paper on the floor. They each then added to this outline artistic representations of their feelings about their body. For example, one student drew a spider web over the top part of the body. They also made three-dimensional newspaper skeletons. Digital photos were then taken of both the body outlines and the model skeletons. These were superimposed over each other using graphics software on the computer. Various effects and filters were applied to explore and develop ideas.

Many of the students in the group found this activity difficult, particularly some of the most artistically gifted, because of their existing knowledge about body structures. However, a student in the group with Down's Syndrome was able to do the activity easily because she had no intellectual concept about the structure of the body. Other students in the group were amazed at what she could do while they were floundering. This helped to integrate her more fully into the group and build relationships. This particular girl used the computer to apply water effects to the superimposed images, representing the hydrotherapy that she had often experienced. This led to further artwork in which she created a mixed-media installation representing herself in water. She used plaster casts to create her body and bleached saris to produce the water effects. In this example ICT acted as part of the process of developing artistic ideas but was not used to create the final piece. However, the developmental work done on the computer was also a piece of art in its own right.

ICT adds another dimension to the work of art students, allowing them to bring images together and act as a stepping-stone to further ideas. ICT provides a means of expressing ideas quickly but is also analytical in the way that students can model ideas. ICT is a completely different medium. Equally importantly, ICT is fun – students are excited about using it. For example, in Year 7, students create simple animations using their own computer drawings, which they really enjoy.

The main challenge for Art has been in carrying the whole department forward with the use of ICT, so that all members have the confidence to use the facilities. This is a slow process – it is best not to rush into it otherwise people get left behind. Our starting point for overcoming this was to bring in an expert in Art and ICT. He was able to show us examples of what schools in the same position were doing and the ideas were innovative and exciting. The ICT team was involved in this training too, which was important, and they have embraced the artistic ideas and helped us to visualise schemes of work and activities involving ICT.

■ Progression in ICT

It is essential for teachers to clearly understand progression within ICT capability if students are to be challenged, especially when ICT skills are acquired in cross-curricular contexts, where most teachers are involved in the planning and teaching of ICT-based activities. Collaboration between subject teachers and ICT specialists as well as the careful design of ICT activities leads to a progression of skills within activities across subject areas. Sometimes a range of levels can be practised and demonstrated within one project. In line with other National Curriculum subjects, nine-level descriptors for ICT capability are provided within the Attainment Target for ICT: 1 to 8 and 'Exceptional Performance'. In the table below these level descriptors have been abbreviated into bullet points for clarity.

Descriptors for ICT capability

Level 1
- Explore different forms of information from various sources.
- Work with text, images and sound to help share ideas.
- Recognise that many everyday devices respond to signals and instructions.
- Make choices when using devices to produce different outcomes.
- Talk about the use of ICT.

Level 2
- Organise and classify information, presenting the findings.
- Generate, amend, save and retrieve work, sharing ideas in different forms.
- Plan and give instructions to make things happen, describing the effects.
- Explore what happens in real and imaginary situations.
- Talk about personal experiences of ICT both inside and outside school.

Level 3
- Save and retrieve work, and search for information using CD-ROMs or the Internet.
- Generate, develop, organise and present work, sharing and exchanging ideas with others.
- Control devices using sets of instructions.
- Make choices and solve problems using models and simulations.
- Describe the use of ICT and its use outside school.

Level 4
■ Search for information by asking careful questions, and check the quality of the results.
■ Combine, edit and present various forms of information, taking the audience into account.
■ Use e-mail to exchange information and ideas with others.
■ Use sensors to collect data from experiments.
■ Investigate patterns and relationships within models, making predictions.
■ Compare the use of ICT with other methods.

Level 5
■ Select information, then check it, organise it and process it.
■ Present information for a range of different purposes and audiences.
■ Exchange information and ideas with others in a variety of ways, including e-mail.
■ Create sets of instructions with care and precision, and use sensors to monitor and measure external events.
■ Explore the effects of changing variables/data within models.
■ Assess the use of ICT within work and identify improvements.

Level 6
■ Improve the quality of work, presenting information from a range of sources in various ways.
■ Test theories using complex searching.
■ Refine sets of instructions to be economical and efficient.
■ Modify the rules within more complex models and compare the results with other observations.
■ Discuss the impact of ICT on society.

Level 7
■ Select, use and interrogate a range of information systems identifying advantages and limitations.
■ Combine information from a range of sources to present to different audiences.
■ Measure, record and analyse physical variables and control events.
■ Design models and procedures with variables.
■ Consider the benefits and limitations of ICT tools and information sources, and discuss their impact on society.

Level 8
■ Select appropriate information sources and ICT tools for specific tasks.
■ Design successful ways to collect and prepare information for processing.
■ Design and implement systems for others to use.
■ Use feedback from sensors to control a system.
■ Discuss social, economic and moral issues raised by ICT.

Exceptional Performance
■ Evaluate software packages and complex computer models, suggesting refinements.
■ Design, implement and document systems for others to use.
■ Relate the experience of information systems to the social, economic, political, legal, ethical and moral issues raised by ICT.

It is equally important that students develop an understanding of what constitutes ICT capability so that they can aim for improvement in their work. At Hampstead School there are two main ways in which this is done. The first is to make the National Curriculum ICT levels explicit within the activities themselves. ICT-based work is then easier to assess, so that if a particular activity is completed successfully, the associated level will have been reached. This helps students to become aware of the progression of skills that leads to more developed ICT capability. The second way to reinforce this awareness is to simplify the level descriptors so that the essential differences or themes are highlighted in a way that students can easily grasp. One interpretation of the key themes that define progression in ICT is shown in Figure 6. ICT can also help to bring about progression within other subject areas, as highlighted in Case study 15.

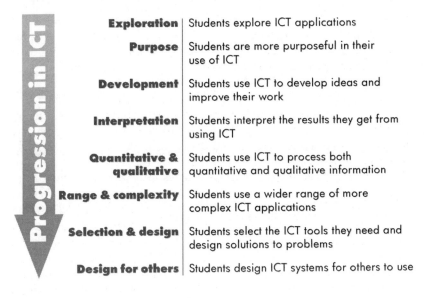

Exploration	Students explore ICT applications
Purpose	Students are more purposeful in their use of ICT
Development	Students use ICT to develop ideas and improve their work
Interpretation	Students interpret the results they get from using ICT
Quantitative & qualitative	Students use ICT to process both quantitative and qualitative information
Range & complexity	Students use a wider range of more complex ICT applications
Selection & design	Students select the ICT tools they need and design solutions to problems
Design for others	Students design ICT systems for others to use

Figure 6 ICT capability – progression

■ Case study 15 – Music

In Music, work with electronic keyboards is introduced early on in Key Stage 3, which gives students basic keyboard skills and an idea of chords and melody in developing compositions. They also have the opportunity to use the Music 2000 software (which will run on a PC or even a Playstation), which is used to introduce structure and texture in music. Students select styles, drumbeats and sounds from libraries in order to create compositions. This approach is very accessible for students as the styles are familiar to them in the music they listen to. In Year 9 they use sequencing software (Cakewalk) to develop their own 'cover version' of Pachebel's 'Canon'. Before doing this they study the classical piece, and versions by The Farm and Puff Daddy. They are given the basic chord sequence as a starting point and they work in pairs to add their own bass line, melody and rhythm. This will lead to creating music for GCSE and A-level compositions in the sequencer (Cubase) from a 'blank sheet'. For A-level Music Technology, students study further sequencing and recording techniques using industry-standard equipment. These uses of ICT operate in parallel with, but do not replace, more traditional approaches to music teaching (for example, classroom instruments, group work, world music etc.).

The user-friendliness of ICT gives a greater number of students a chance to create music – opening it up to everybody. You only have to see the expressions on the students' faces to see that they have achieved something in the lesson that they did not think they could do. They can make music without having to read a note of it. In the past, students could only compose if they played an instrument, because they could play and hear what they had written. ICT can help both instrument players and non-instrumentalists by providing immediate playback, which can later be performed from a printed score. While we still want to encourage violinists and pianists, the use of ICT helps to challenge an elitist view of music and supports an expanding music industry where a range of different musical skills are equally valued. ICT increases critical awareness of music by allowing the immediate listening and appraising of composition work. Technology is broadening the whole concept of performance – DJ-ing and mixing allow more students to reach high levels of performance skill.

One of the greatest challenges in using ICT within Music is the 'blank sheet of paper'. The aim is for students to compose original pieces of music, and by Key Stage 4 students need to be able to come up with compositional ideas. However, lower down the school some of the worst music lessons for us have been when students are given total creative freedom. The best ones are more structured, where the students are given an idea to work on (such as the Pachebel activity) without suppressing creativity. The progression from highly structured to increasingly open-ended opportunities helps to resolve the 'blank sheet of paper' problem. Also, students often work in pairs or small groups, feeding ideas off each other and evaluating and appraising each others' work. Equipment is another challenge. However, small but adequate MIDI keyboards, the same size as the computer keyboard, and headphones plugged into 'splitters' have enabled a whole class to use the sequencing software in pairs at the same time.

■ Conclusion

In breaking down ICT capability into strands, both in terms of types of applications and the processes involved in using them, the place of ICT within the National Curriculum becomes clearer. ICT capability is not just about the acquisition of computer skills, it is also about using ICT as a tool for learning. The process skills that comprise the newly-defined strands of ICT capability can be applied using a wide range of applications across all curriculum areas, with the aim of enhancing learning within each subject. This is particularly relevant at Key Stage 4, by which time students should be able to 'use ICT to enhance their learning and the quality of their work... tackling demanding problems in a wide variety of contexts, including work in other subjects' (DfEE/QCA, 1999, pp. 22–3). The processes of ICT capability and some of the ways in which they can lead to subject enhancement are shown in Figure 7. This role of ICT in improving subject teaching and learning is fundamental to the cross-curricular approach to ICT, which is considered more fully in Chapter 7.

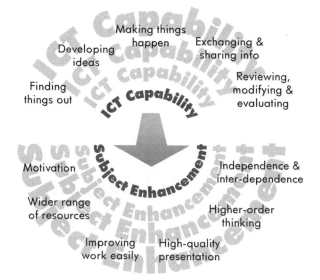

Figure 7 ICT capability – leading to subject enhancement

▆▆▆ Main points

■ ICT capability is defined within the National Curriculum.

■ ICT capability involves hands-on, practical skills.

■ ICT capability can be usefully broken down into strands, viewed as either applications or processes.

■ Teachers and students need to understand the progression of skills that comprise ICT capability.

■ ICT capability is also about knowing when and how to use ICT effectively as a tool for learning across the curriculum.

7 A cross-curricular approach to ICT

'Pupils should be given opportunities to apply and develop their ICT capability through the use of ICT tools to support their learning in all subjects.'

(DfEE/QCA, 1999, p. 36)

There can be no doubt that schools are expected to integrate the use of ICT into all parts of the curriculum – the extract from the National Curriculum (above) is a legal requirement. However, this is not an easy requirement to meet. There are implications for resources, staff expertise, timetabling and technical support. OFSTED findings are not favourable: 'good work often occurs in designated information technology lessons, but it is insufficiently integrated with applications of information technology in other subjects' (OFSTED 2000, paragraph 108). One of the main problems for schools has been the perceived need to teach ICT as a subject in its own right while at the same time trying to integrate ICT into the curriculum. Advice on the matter, some of which is outlined below, has been at best ambiguous. In this chapter some different curriculum models for meeting the demands of ICT in the National Curriculum are considered, before looking more closely at the cross-curricular approach adopted by Hampstead School.

Curriculum models for ICT

Several models for the delivery of ICT capability in secondary schools have emerged. In most cases, there is a balance between the teaching of ICT as a *discrete* subject in its own right, and the *cross-curricular* development of ICT capability within other curriculum subjects. The non-statutory guidance accompanying the initial National Curriculum orders (NCC, 1990, p. C2) stated that 'the IT programmes of study are best taught through other subjects'. However, fulfilling this recommendation was not helped by the organisation of the National Curriculum. The programmes of study and attainment targets for IT (as it was then) were initially subsumed in the Technology orders alongside Design and Technology, which was an established secondary subject area. Many schools at this time also had well-developed, if small, departments for teaching computer-based courses at GCSE and advanced levels. Taken together, these factors sent rather ambiguous messages to schools: IT was firmly placed within the Technology curriculum, away from any existing specialist IT departments, but the recommended delivery model was cross-curricular.

The Dearing review of the National Curriculum recognised the mistake of 'hiding' IT within Technology and the revised orders for IT (DFE, 1995) were published separately. There was also a statutory 'common requirement' that 'pupils should be given opportunities, where appropriate, to develop and apply their IT capability in their study of National Curriculum subjects' (DFE, 1995, *Information Technology in the National Curriculum* page 1). This requirement was supported by non-statutory guidance (SCAA, 1995) setting out a range of ways in which IT could be used within other subjects. The revised National Curriculum for 2000 (DfEE/QCA, 1999) has strengthened the requirement for the integration of ICT into the wider curriculum via statutory references to ICT within each subject's orders. At the same time the Key Stage 3 scheme of work for ICT has been published, providing detailed 'units' of work. This scheme of work is likely to be easier to implement within a discrete course (although making use of it is not a statutory requirement). So once again the message to schools is mixed in terms of how ICT teaching should be organised.

In arguing for some discrete teaching of ICT it is sometimes stated that students need to be taught some ICT skills in isolation before they can usefully apply them within their other subjects. This also helps to ensure that all students are taught a basic ICT curriculum and assessment procedures can be implemented in the usual way. It is difficult to achieve full coverage of the ICT orders solely through a cross-curricular approach. Major issues need tackling, including planning, progression, assessment, staff development and access to resources. Also, because subject and department-based teaching is the norm in secondary schools, in many cases ICT is still treated as a subject in its own right. These factors, along with the tendency in secondary schools to put anything that needs to be taught on the timetable, has led many schools to adopt a 'hybrid' (Crawford, 1997, p. 14) combination of discrete teaching and cross-curricular integration. It is important to note that a school following the discrete approach alone would not be meeting its statutory obligations. However, the hybrid model also presents major problems. Few secondary schools are sufficiently well resourced or staffed with ICT specialists to prevent separate ICT lessons and cross-curricular ICT work detracting from each other. Both ICT resources and the ICT teachers' time become preoccupied with 'ICT lessons', and little access and support is available for cross-curricular work. This is magnified when the school offers ICT-related GCSE or post-16 options. Such courses allow a few students who are interested in ICT to further their knowledge and skills to high levels, but this is usually at the expense of the rest. Furthermore, there is a danger that ICT becomes the preserve of the ICT 'department' and other staff feel that they cannot or need not become involved. The hybrid approach is therefore self-defeating: by attempting both to teach ICT as a subject and also to integrate it into the curriculum neither can be done effectively.

Some schools, like Hampstead School, have chosen to remove ICT almost entirely from the timetabled curriculum, freeing up resources and the ICT specialists' time to enable ICT capability to be fully integrated into the curriculum. As Birnbaum (1990, p. 29) has explained, 'the curriculum becomes for the pupil a seed-bed for IT applications'. A programme of cross-curricular ICT activities needs to be established involving ongoing liaison and planning with subject teachers. The underlying belief is that the curriculum itself can supply the most meaningful contexts in which to *learn* ICT skills as well as *apply* them. It is sometimes argued (Crawford, 1997, p. 13) that this is an 'expensive' approach, because team-teaching is often involved. However, value for money needs to be judged broadly. If the cross-curricular approach is working effectively, students are developing ICT capability in a meaningful context and their subject learning is enhanced. But there is also a vital, two-way staff development function being served. Through teamwork the ICT specialists gain a clearer understanding of subject requirements, and subject teachers receive ongoing ICT training and support in situ. Dwyer (1994) has stated that 'six years of research reveals that microcomputers and other interactive educational technologies are most powerfully used in learning activities where children are engaged in tasks with real purpose.' The integrated, cross-curricular approach provides the 'real purpose' that students need when using ICT.

■ The guiding principles of cross-curricular ICT

As shown in Figure 8, there are four main principles underpinning the cross-curricular approach to ICT at Hampstead School:

- entitlement;

- enhancement;

- access;

- support.

It is a legal requirement, set out in the National Curriculum, for schools to provide opportunities for the acquisition of ICT capability as an entitlement for all students. Schools also have a statutory obligation to develop ways of using ICT across the curriculum to bring about subject enhancement. Within a fully cross-curricular approach, students' only formal ICT experiences occur within a range of 'host' subjects, so entitlement and enhancement go hand in hand. To achieve this, staff and students need to be able to access ICT facilities and their own ICT work as easily as possible. ICT rooms need to be available during lesson times so that classes can be booked in, and supervised for open access at other times. Adequate access to resources and storage space really means networked computers, with individual user accounts for staff and students. Support is also needed from the ICT specialists within the school so that students and staff get the help, encouragement and training they need.

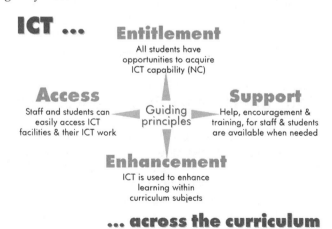

Figure 8 A cross-curricular approach to ICT – guiding principles

The principles of entitlement, enhancement, access and support should be central to the school's ICT policy (see Appendix 1), and need to be clearly stated. They also lead to the key questions for monitoring and evaluating the whole-school ICT programme. The tests to apply when looking at the effectiveness of a particular ICT activity should be:

■ Has learning been enhanced within the host subject?

■ Has ICT capability been extended?

It is important that all concerned – subject teachers, ICT staff and students – are in agreement about the answers to these questions before any conclusions are drawn. If the answers to both questions are 'no', then the activity should be scrapped. If the answer to either of the questions is 'no', then some more work needs to be done in developing the activity. There is no shame involved in deciding that things do not work and need improving. On the contrary, reflective and self-critical practice among teachers is the only way to ensure that improvements take place. Most teachers, quite rightly, are only willing to integrate ICT into their subject teaching if it brings about a perceived learning enhancement. Similarly, it is the job of ICT staff to ensure that, as far as possible, students are furthering their ICT capability and not just repeating what has been done in other subjects. One of the inherent problems of the cross-curricular approach is that sometimes the ICT gets in the way of the subject teaching, and vice versa – a phenomenon that has been well-named 'interference' (Birnbaum, 1990, p. 33). The inverse of interference is enhancement (shown in Figure 9), where ICT teaching and subject teaching are mutually beneficial. ICT capability is acquired and extended in a meaningful context, while subject-based learning is motivated and reinforced by the use of ICT. It is the role of the ICT team, considered in more detail in Chapter 8, to help bring about a shift from interference to enhancement.

From interference to enhancement

When evaluating ICT activities, different levels of enhancement can be identified. In most cases, at the very least, increased student motivation is observed when ICT is being used. Frequently, it is clear that the use of ICT has enabled students to improve the quality of their presentations. Often, ICT can free students from otherwise very laborious tasks and allow them to concentrate on the concepts and skills underlying the particular area of study. Sometimes the use of ICT can lead to a greater understanding or grasp of a particular topic, concept

From interference

To enhancement

From interference	To enhancement
Subject	
• Hardware is unreliable • Software is too complex or difficult to learn • Software is new & unfamiliar • Quality of information is mixed or poor	• ICT promotes a range of active learning styles • Basic tasks done quickly make time for higher-order work • Work is easy to improve • ICT & subject skills are complementary
ICT	
• ICT skills do not move beyond the trivial • Use of ICT is repetitive • ICT is only used for drill & practice or demonstration • Limited scope for assessing ICT capability	• ICT capability is developed in a meaningful context • ICT skills are extended • Built-in progression of ICT skills facilitates assessment • Subject teachers gain ICT skills alongside students

Role of ICT team ➤

Figure 9 A cross-curricular approach to ICT – enhancement

or skill, because of the way in which it has been presented and developed. Occasionally the use of ICT enables learners to see something in a way that they have not experienced before and perhaps would not have experienced at all without the influence of ICT. This last type of enhancement is almost magical, and is a very personal experience (like Papert's gears in Chapter 4) in the sense that others could find similar 'inspiration' in different circumstances or with different resources. In all of these levels of enhancement, the quality of learning may not be attributable to the use of ICT alone. It will be determined by the particular set of factors that make up the teaching–learning situation, of which ICT is just one. Further examples of the ways in which ICT can enhance learning are provided in *IT Works: Stimulate to Educate* (Brown and Howlett, 1994), and are listed in the table on page 90.

The ICT programme at Hampstead School

There are ample opportunities within the range of subject areas to promote ICT capability, and for ICT to make an impact on subject teaching and learning. Like most schools following a cross-curricular approach, Hampstead School is primarily concerned with developing

Ways in which ICT can enhance learning (Brown and Howlett, 1994)

1. Children who use a computer at home are more enthusiastic and confident when using one in school.
2. Video games can be educational if they are well managed.
3. IT can provide a safe and non-threatening environment for learning.
4. IT has the flexibility to meet the needs and abilities of each student.
5. Students who do not enjoy learning can be encouraged by the use of IT.
6. Computers give students the chance to achieve where they have previously failed.
7. Computers can reduce the risk of failure at school.
8. IT lets students reflect on what they have written and change it easily.
9. Using a computer to produce a successful piece of writing can motivate students to acquire basic literacy skills.
10. IT gives students immediate access to richer source materials.
11. IT can present information in new ways which help students to understand, assimilate and read it more readily.
12. IT removes the chore of processing data manually and frees students to concentrate on its interpretation and use.
13. Difficult ideas are made more understandable when information technology makes them visible.
14. Interactive technology motivates and stimulates learning.
15. Computing programs which use digitised speech can help students to read and spell.
16. IT gives students the power to try out different ideas and to take risks.
17. Computer simulations encourage analytical and divergent thinking.
18. IT is particularly successful in holding the attention of pupils with emotional and behavioural difficulties.
19. IT can often compensate for the communication and learning difficulties of students with physical and sensory impairments.
20. Pupils with profound and multiple learning difficulties can be encouraged to purposeful activity and self-awareness by IT.
21. Using IT makes teachers take a fresh look at how they teach and the ways in which students learn.
22. Computers help students to learn when used in well-designed, meaningful tasks and activities.
23. Students make more effective use of computers if teachers know how and why to intervene.
24. IT offers potential for effective group working.
25. Giving teachers easy access to computers encourages and improves the use of IT in the curriculum.
26. Head teachers using computers raise the profile of IT in their schools.
27. Management Information Systems can save time and money in schools.

a range of ICT experiences for students that meet the statutory require-ments of the National Curriculum and make a positive contribution to the subjects in which they occur. It is important to ensure that all the strands of ICT capability can be developed and that progress can be made to increasingly advanced and autonomous skills. Some examples of cross-curricular ICT activities are set out below. Others can be found in the cross-curricular ICT map (see Appendix 3). A cross-curricular ICT map provides a useful overview of what goes on where, and repre-sents a 'snapshot' of the considerable collaborative and developmental work that goes on between subject specialists and ICT staff. The nature of the cross-curricular approach means that the ICT map is ever-changing – new ICT activities are being developed all the time, as new software becomes available or when a new idea is followed-up.

In English, Year 7 students produce poems and newspaper articles using a wordprocessor. Suitable graphics are added to illustrate the text and the needs of the audience are considered. These skills are built upon in History during Year 9, when students report on an event from the past from a particular viewpoint. For example, a wide range of sources, including books, CD-ROMs and the Internet, are used to gather information on events in Little Rock when schools became desegregated in the 1960s. These are synthesised into a newspaper page, which is reorganised and formatted in a variety of ways to achieve an optimal layout. Students also apply presentation skills using wordprocessing and graphics software in French and Spanish. For example, they produce a 'wanted' poster describing the features of an imaginary criminal, adding a photo-fit style cartoon graphic assembled on the screen. In Music, students use multi-track sequencing software to develop a basic chord sequence they have been given, adding drum tracks, bass lines and melodies to arrive at different musical styles (see Case study 15 in Chapter 6).

Data-handling skills are first developed in Maths, where students build a database of information about themselves, which they later interrogate using simple and complex searching, sorting and graphing techniques. More complex graphs are created in Geography during a study of population growth using data gathered from the Internet. The graphs are imported into a wordprocessor for interpretation and description. The Internet is also used in Modern Languages for e-mail and video conferencing with a school in France. Students have commu-nicated with their French counterparts in both English and French and they have attached digital pictures, sounds and videos to some of their messages. The following case study describes some of the benefits to language learning of these activities, as well as some of the issues involved in running an e-mail club.

■ Case study 16 – Modern Languages

There are numerous benefits from using ICT in the modern foreign languages lesson, ranging from improving access to the curriculum for a broad range of abilities, to enhancing experimentation with all four language skills. Moreover, the e-mail club is gradually becoming an invaluable tool to the teacher's repertoire, greatly benefiting language learning for the simplest of reasons – it is making the whole experience very real:

> *'With the club, we can talk to French people of our own age, and we can relate*
> *better.'*   (Year 9 student)

At the club, students constantly focus on communicating with their peers in a variety of exciting ways. They could be listening to their voices and providing oral responses in return, or reading personalised correspondence addressed to them in a foreign language. They write back with the knowledge that the conversation carries on through a virtual dialogue, generating excitement and drive among the learners. Video links and colourful digital pictures further enhance the process of improving language skills as well as motivation. In the longer term, many club members hope to meet their penpal for real!

The range of abilities represented in the e-mail club indicates that students in general and low-attainers in particular are keen to participate in what is a voluntary extra-curricular activity. More than just going to the ICT room to do some work as part of their French lesson, these students are developing a special connection with someone in France which only belongs to them. Even if they end up writing some English in their messages, they are communicating in a fun way, enhancing literacy skills and taking part in a positive, exciting and inclusive experience, which provides an opportunity for success in language learning. At the same time, high fliers have more opportunity to explore with the foreign language and recycle previous knowledge that might be otherwise under-utilised.

The fast-track learning experience for such students corresponds to what many professional linguists believe – that real exposure to a language and increased practice are the determining factors in the rapid progress of these students. The e-mail club provides the extra degree of motivation and exposure that can make the difference. 'Virtual' learning can help to achieve teaching goals regarding differentiation at all levels. It also provides the necessary motivation to inclusive and successful language learning.

Another tangible benefit for students who have a direct contact with a French person of their own age is appreciating other children's culture, schooling and everyday life. It develops their international and cultural awareness and enables them to talk about their own lives – something they love to do:

'I really like to learn what they do when it is Christmas and we told them what is Halloween.' (Year 9 student)

Beyond common constraints, such as ICT training or resource availability, running an e-mail club entails a series of careful considerations and one needs to be fully prepared to avoid pitfalls. The teacher needs to make sure that the partner correspondent organisation has an ICT capacity compatible with the home school. A key factor is to keep students motivated on an ongoing basis. A partner school that could not match the digital facilities, for example, could not send images back, and this would work against the spontaneity and excitement of virtual learning. It is also important to be in direct and regular contact with a key teacher in the partner school.

Matching pupils' levels well is important since they are going to establish an ongoing exchange with their designated peers. Teachers need to share information about their pupils before matching them. Ideally, students should be of a similar age, language levels need to be reconciled to ensure good communication, and common interests or hobbies could be taken into account. At the same time, it is useful to retain a degree of flexibility when pairing penpals. If a serious and committed member of the club requests two virtual friends and shows the motivation and ability to cope, this can prove beneficial.

If the aim is to communicate mainly in the target language, it is important to teach students how to access reference sources such as dictionaries via the computer. However, using English as part of the communication process is an important success factor. Indeed, students of the partner school wish to receive documents in their target language. In return our students get messages in French or Spanish, which benefits their foreign language acquisition.

Running an e-mail club is proving to be real fun and real hard work. Its successes are largely due to children's enthusiasm and supportive ICT experts who are gradually building everybody's confidence in the field. We all become more expert day by day. This ICT activity is a very rewarding and positive learning experience for all:

'In the class you have to repeat things and it can get boring, but in the club it's like having a conversation!' (Year 9 student)

In Design and Technology, there are opportunities for more extended ICT projects (see Case study 11 in Chapter 5). In Year 7, students develop flow-chart systems to control model traffic lights and pelican crossings. In Year 8, more complex systems are designed to control sliding door and lift models. Computer-assisted design (CAD) packages are also used in Design and Technology to carry out a range of tasks including packaging designs for CDs and chocolate bars, and also technical floorplans. The use of computer-assisted manufacturing (CAM) equipment is also being introduced into the Design and Technology curriculum. Different graphical skills are developed in Art, for example, where students are given a digital black and white version of a famous painting to develop using colour schemes taken from expressionist paintings. Mood can be modelled by selecting different portions of the image and applying colour (see Case study 14 in Chapter 6).

Data-logging activities are mainly carried out in Science, where different sensors are used to capture, plot and analyse temperature, sound and light data for a range of experiments. Another opportunity for data-logging is offered in PE, where students can monitor their own pulse rates with portable sensors during physical activities. The data is stored within these sensors and can be later transferred to a computer for analysis. Simple modelling programs are used in Maths to explore transformations of shapes and to build tessellations. These modelling skills are developed in Maths using spreadsheets and LOGO until students are designing their own models for simple accounting purposes and using LOGO procedures with variables to generate shapes (see Case study 13 in Chapter 5). Modelling programs such as Crocodile Clips are used in Science to create virtual electrical circuits, which can be tested before building them using real components (see Case study 12 in Chapter 5).

The structure of the ICT programme at Hampstead School is summarised in Figures 10 and 11. In Key Stage 3, students build a portfolio of evidence for the activities, in both electronic form in their network user areas and in paper form in a centrally stored folder. At the end of Year 9, these are formally assessed to arrive at an end of Key Stage 3 National Curriculum level. As students move into Key Stage 4, they are expected to use ICT more autonomously in producing coursework for their GCSE subjects. Set pieces of work from across the curriculum contribute to an ICT portfolio, which is used to accredit their ICT capability using the stand-alone key skills unit. An Advanced Vocational A level course is available for post-16 students wishing to specialise in ICT or combine ICT with their other studies in Year 12 as an AS level. In Year 13, the optional units are matched, as far as

ICT activities
- Integrated into most subjects' schemes of work
- Done by all students to form *ICT entitlement*
- Designed collaboratively by ICT staff and subject staff
- Designed to teach ICT capability & enhance subject learning
- Timetabled in advance to ensure access & support

Independent study
- Students encouraged to use ICT to improve work & enhance learning
- SuccessMaker, CD-ROMs, Internet access, ICT tools

ICT assessment
- ICT levels built into activities
- Portfolio of ICT work built during KS3, electronic & hard copy
- Level of ICT capability awarded & reported at end of Year 9

ICT Key stage 3 programme

Figure 10 A cross-curricular approach to ICT – key stage 3

Key stage 4 & post-16 ICT programme

ICT across the curriculum
- More autonomous use of ICT to support studies
- Subject-specific ICT activities & use of ICT for coursework

Certification of ICT skills
- Stand-alone ICT Key Skills accreditation for all KS4 & Post-16 students at the appropriate level
- *National Interaction Computing Award Scheme (NICAS)* also available for application-based skills

ICT vocational A level
- Single (3 unit AS) & part (6 unit A2) awards offered
- Optional units matched to students' other studies to extend the cross-curricular approach

Figure 11 A cross-curricular approach to ICT – key stage 4 and post-16

possible, with students' interests and other subjects. This is in keeping with the whole-school, cross-curricular approach to ICT as a tool for learning. Other post-16 students continue to use ICT independently and within their subjects, and are entered for the key skills unit at a higher level. In Case study 17, one student describes her own, increasingly autonomous use of ICT.

■ Case study 17 – A student's development

I am currently pursuing my academic career in the Sixth Form at Hampstead School, through Media Studies, English and Design & Technology. My first encounter with the computer came at around the age of seven, playing keyboard games with my best friend (of course Nintendo and Sega came before, but they don't really count). Following that was at my first secondary school, where we would all exchange a long list of secret codes to enter into the lunchtime and after-school world of a special computer game. When I left the school, the mystery of the codes stayed!

At Hampstead, the computer was no longer a playful device; it became a tool towards success and respect. The first real challenge was with GCSE Design and Technology. My coursework project involved the designing and making of a flyer with a free gift. Drawing the image to go behind the text was simple, except I made the whole process unnecessarily long by drawing black ink onto rainbow-coloured paper. After the black and white photocopy was scanned into the computer, there were different shades of grey left to clean up. Slowly and gradually, with the assistance of ICT support staff, I began to learn about the different tools in Adobe PhotoShop and CorelDraw. The image eventually became filled with variants of gradient colour, which were hard to decide upon. Text was separately attached to the image with acetate and my first creation was born. Recently, the same design launched a real club-night. I plan to create more and more images for flyers on the computer and use them for my growing business to become a greater success.

For the first module of A level Media Studies, the class were assigned the production of a horror movie, which involved creating a film poster for promotion. All the students produced amazing images based on the typical horror stereotype with eerie woods and cemeteries. I decided to take my ideas further. Digital images of my younger sisters and their friends dressed in cloaks and hoods, making gory faces, were taken and transferred to my computer files, after which I began to create the images of spirits, by swirling and distorting the original pictures. I added a plastic effect and made the images a bit transparent, then softened them into the background.

Lots of problems arose for different reasons. For example, the file space was limited and work had to be wiped off and re-started. The original image I wanted to scan was unobtainable and so I had to negotiate with an alternative background, destroying the original perspective of the image. The end product, however, was presentable and reached all the recommendations of a film poster with a website address too, which supports the contemporary standard of computer technology used within my production company.

Moving away from the school environment, I have completed the production and design of the U.K.R.C.M.P. logo, which is a symbol for complementary medicine in the United Kingdom. The production had tight deadlines to meet, which were made difficult through the lack of accessibility to a computer within the school. There were several occasions when I needed to finish a particular stage of the logo, but the computer room had been closed to students or the school was shutting early.

The overall image was not difficult to design; the only problem was that I would sometimes forget a specific set-up of tools in a program, for example, fitting texts onto a particular path, in this case a curve. Achieving the correct positioning of the text was not easy. There was always a complication and I needed to be reminded of the particular tool used. This is now one of my most practised and effective tools in CorelDraw. The logo involved the use of the digital camera as well as a steady hand to trace around the combined images with the paintbrush tool in CorelPhotoPaint. Another time-consuming problem was in the overlay of shapes which was used to achieve the desired effect of a sun and moon within a circle outline of the logo. It took a lot of experimenting before the procedure was completed.

I have now gained respect within the school and local environment and this has been with the aid of computer technology. Without computer technology, my organisational, designing and conversational skills would not be recognised. The computer has been used for many other personal and academic projects I have undertaken, including poetry with text over elaborate images as well as poetry in simple black and white text, design assignments, business cards, formal letters, typing my curriculum vitae, e-mail, Internet access, etc. As it progresses and becomes more efficient, the computer will continue to be important to my future!

■ Conclusion

It is important to stress that the activities described in this chapter comprise a 'snapshot' of the cross-curricular ICT programme at Hampstead School at the time of writing. It represents 'work in progress' and not 'work completed'. There is much to do in improving the programme: developing new activities and projects, making progression across subjects and key stages more coherent, making students more aware of the ICT processes they experience and how they benefit learning, providing better assessment and accreditation of ICT capability. The need for continual improvement and the rapid change inherent in the technology itself together mean that 'work is never finished'. But any project aimed at school development will entail ongoing change. Schools that are both 'effective' and 'improving' are characterised by Stoll and Fink (1996, pp. 85–6) as 'moving schools', where staff are 'actively working together to respond to their changing context and to keep developing'. Rising to this challenge is the most exciting aspect of managing ICT across the curriculum, and this is the subject of Chapter 8.

■ Main points

- It is a statutory requirement for ICT to be used across the curriculum.

- A cross-curricular approach enables ICT capability to be acquired and developed in real, meaningful contexts.

- An effective cross-curricular approach allows ICT to enhance learning within a range of subjects.

- Cross-curricular ICT activities should be reviewed critically.

- The cross-curricular ICT map continually changes.

8 Managing ICT across the curriculum

'The crux of the matter is getting the right people talking together on a regular basis with the right information at their disposal.'

(Fullan, 1992, p. 87)

The cross-curricular approach to ICT, like many whole-school initiatives, works if teachers are willing to get involved and if the ICT specialists in the school are able to support them. Policies, development plans and schemes of work, considered later in this chapter, are undoubtedly important in shaping practice, but ultimately it is the involvement and collaboration of staff that gets things done. The first step in managing ICT across the curriculum is to establish a group of ICT specialists within the school who act as a support team rather than as a traditional department. This may initially appear a rather cosmetic distinction, but it has proved to be a key to effective collaboration.

The ICT team

At Hampstead School the ICT team works with all staff and departments to develop ICT activities that are designed to meet two fundamental aims:

- the enhancement of subject teaching and learning;
- the acquisition of ICT capability.

As explained in the previous chapter, the fundamental role of the ICT team is to remove any potential interference to both the acquisition of ICT capability and learning enhancement within a particular subject. This is made easier by refusing to treat ICT in the traditional way – as a 'subject' with an associated 'department'. Instead, ICT is viewed as a tool for teaching, learning and management that everyone in the school can and should be using effectively. The ICT team needs to be led by someone with status in the school, preferably a member of the

Senior Management Team, so that a whole-school vision and strategy for ICT can be articulated. The support of the Governors, Headteacher and Senior Management Team is crucial in creating the expectation that ICT is an issue for everyone in the school. The ICT team also needs members whose teaching is rooted within other subjects, particularly from large departments such as Maths, English and Science. This leads to 'localised' co-ordination of ICT within the core subjects, with greater ownership and integration of ICT within each department. The ICT co-ordinators in each subject area also become part of a whole-school team, which contributes to their own professional development. Other essential members of the ICT team are a cross-curricular co-ordinator to work with the smaller departments, and network/system management and technical staff to keep the technology running smoothly. In addition, ICT support staff are required to help staff and students in their day-to-day use of ICT for teaching, learning and administrative purposes.

A great deal of ongoing work is required by the ICT team to keep ICT integrated: revising existing ICT activities, developing new opportunities for using ICT, exploring new technologies, furthering the skills of new and existing teachers. The following case study describes one use of ICT within the History curriculum and the way in which it was improved through collaboration between History teachers and members of the ICT team.

■ Case study 17 – History

One of the ICT activities we do in History involves the analysis of primary material on living and working conditions during the Industrial Revolution. Census data covering the Coalbrookdale area is provided in a database that students can interrogate by searching, sorting and graphing. The activity is a means of extension and reinforcement after the main concepts have been introduced in the classroom. The key question for students is: 'What questions could be asked of this source, and how do we get the answers?' In structuring suitable questions, students are involved in a process of trial and error.

There are many benefits in using ICT to carry out this activity. At the beginning of the lesson the students are shown a hard-copy version of the data set, a huge bundle of paper containing 1500 records. Students can readily appreciate the problems of working with that volume of data, as it roughly corresponds to the number of students in the school. Students are also asked to spend a few minutes browsing through the data before using the analysis tools within the software.

The time-saving power of ICT for counting, sorting, searching and graphing the data becomes very apparent. There is a close link between the ICT skills and the History skills involved in such an activity, in terms of the gathering of information and the awareness of the audience in presenting it.

There were also challenges involved in making the best use of ICT for this activity. At first, some of the questions that were asked of the data were not really giving us the answers we wanted. Also some of the selection processes involved were very repetitive, leading to little progression in either ICT skills or History understanding. The activity was restructured to avoid repetition of skills and to address more directly the historical issues. In carrying out this review of the activity another previously unnoticed historical dimension became apparent – the issue of gender. The role of women is an important ongoing historical theme, and the divisions in Britain during the Industrial Revolution were clearly highlighted by gender analysis of the census data.

Both ICT and History staff were pleased with the revision to the Coalbrookdale activity, arrived at through collaboration. From the ICT point of view, progression to more advanced skills, including complex searching, was made possible. For History, the analysis of historical evidence led to higher order thinking and interpretation skills, as students were faced with the question: 'Why do you think this is so?'

The model of an ICT team described above and shown in Figure 12 may appear 'unreal'. In practice the same person often performs several jobs, which is certainly the case at Hampstead School. However, the key roles for the whole-school management of ICT are identified, which may provide a useful blueprint for an ideal staffing structure. Lines of communication between members of the team are vital (easier if all the roles are shared between a few people), but they need not necessarily be via formal meetings. In fact at Hampstead School, meetings of the whole ICT team have proved unwieldy, as each member of the team brings a set of needs specific to their own situation, only some of which need to be shared with the group. Whole team meetings are held occasionally or as and when necessary, to discuss major issues such as development planning, policy making, resourcing and training. Regular, ongoing meetings between smaller subsets of the ICT team (often just pairs) are more fruitful and effective in dealing with immediate concerns. The ICT leader acts as a channel for communication between all the team members and important information can be passed on in a variety of formal and informal ways.

The ICT team ...

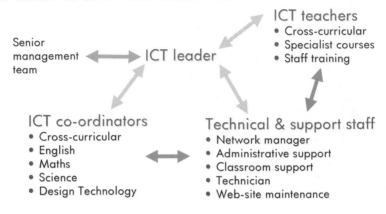

Figure 12 Managing ICT across the curriculum – the ICT team

■ Monitoring and evaluating ICT across the curriculum

Another function of the ICT leader is to monitor and evaluate the way in which departments use ICT, leading to ongoing revision and improvement of the ICT programme by the ICT team. The key questions that guide monitoring and evaluation were discussed in the previous chapter:

- Has subject learning been enhanced through the use of ICT?

- Has ICT capability been extended?

These rather general questions can be answered at an instinctive, professional level by subject teachers and ICT specialists together. However, North (1990, pp. 25–7) provides a useful and more detailed checklist of thirteen questions for 'identifying quality in the cross-curricular use of IT', and these are set out in the table below. These questions highlight many of the cross-curricular ICT issues raised in this book. It is unlikely that for any given ICT activity the answer to all of these questions will be 'yes'. Nevertheless, applied to a school's ICT programme as a whole, they provide an excellent framework for 'quality control'.

Identifying quality in the cross-curricular use of IT (North, 1990)

1. Is the experience purposeful, meaningful, relevant and meeting real needs?
2. Is the experience largely practical?
3. Do pupils experience active involvement with IT?
4. Do pupils experience co-operative working situations?
5. Do pupils experience the freedom that can be gained from fully autonomous work?
6. Do pupils experience the involvement of the teacher as a participant?
7. Does the experience promote discussion and oracy?
8. Do pupils experience an interactive approach to work?
9. Does the experience lead to a transfer of competencies and knowledge?
10. Does the experience aid the acquisition of skills of using information appropriately?
11. Does assessment support the process of the experience?
12. Does the experience encourage higher order conceptual activity?
13. Are the pupils' experiences progressive?

▌ Managing ICT resources

The procurement and management of ICT resources is another major role of the ICT team. Many schools now have multi-server networks with several hundred stations, serving over a thousand users. This represents an ICT infrastructure that is comparable in size to a fairly large business or a small higher education establishment. These types of organisation commonly have whole teams of ICT staff to oversee the running of networks and to support users in a variety of ways. Schools are fortunate to have one suitably qualified ICT technician, and technical tasks are frequently carried out by ICT teachers. There are nearly always several items of ICT equipment to repair or replace, software to be upgraded or installed, new users to be registered and consumables to be provided. Schools have the added wear and tear created by the presence of young people, such as missing mouse balls, grubby keyboards and forgotten passwords. As well as basic maintenance tasks, there is a range of developmental jobs to be done, as listed in Figure 13.

ICT requires management ...

Maintenance tasks:

- Management of user accounts
- Changing passwords
- Performing routine repairs
- Repair/replacement of faulty items
- Provision of consumables
- Renewal of maintenance contracts
- Updating equipment inventory
- Monitoring network usage
- Checking status of servers
- Carrying out backup procedures
- Updating critical software, e.g. new drivers, anti-virus protection

Development tasks:

- Ordering new resources
- Installing & testing new hardware & software
- Liasing with ICT providers
- Building a local knowledge-base for solving problems
- Familiarisation with new resources
- Passing on necessary technical expertise to teaching staff
- Providing technical user support
- Keeping up-to-date with new technologies

... this requires people

Figure 13 Managing ICT across the curriculum – resources

Organisation and management of networks requires careful consideration. In order to meet ever-changing needs networks need to be developed, and to maximise their potential some calculated risks need to be taken. Upgrading or adding new hardware or software, changing configurations, and improving cabling topologies can all potentially disrupt normal service, but careful planning can usually minimise 'down-time'. To meet these demands schools need technicians and network managers with considerable skills, skills that can attract much higher salaries in the private sector.

To overcome the difficulty in recruiting suitably skilled staff, 'managed services' are now being offered to schools by many of the educational ICT suppliers, whereby certain system management tasks are delegated to external specialists. Nevertheless, the requirement for some in-house technical back-up cannot be overstated. While there may be specific tasks for which schools will want to buy-in expertise – such as cabling and server commissioning – the continual needs arising within a large school demand the presence of permanent on-site technical support. One solution to these problems that Hampstead School has pursued has been the employment of ex-students as technical support staff. These posts have begun as work experience placements, and have been extended to full employment after a period of 'settling-in' has elapsed, and when job descriptions and funding have been properly identified. The case study below provides an account of one member of staff who was employed in this way.

▇ Case study 18 – ICT Network Manager and Support

My interest in computers expanded as I began learning and under-standing more about their uses while I was a student at Hampstead School. My knowledge grew from helping out after school, formatting disks and printing display work, into helping in and out of lessons. Even while I was at college I would come back to help with the IT CPVE course. I became familiar with the networks at the school and was able to trouble-shoot a variety of problems from software to printing and even hardware problems.

I started working at Hampstead School in September 1992 when I was offered a temporary job as technician. I spent a lot of time learning on the job – as you do. I was fortunate to have started working at the school while they were implementing a new network. This gave me even more opportunity to watch and learn from engineers who came on site to commission servers and implement other upgrades.

Supporting staff has been difficult, and it has meant learning most of the software while providing training. Trying to pitch myself at the right level has always been a worry because you can either come across too technical or patronising. Having seen many changes in how the school approaches ICT, I now know the key to the use of ICT is support, as without it the whole system just collapses. I have seen a major increase in the use of ICT in the last four years, and a lot of the students coming into the school know more about the software than I do. They can be a good resource for finding weaknesses in the network and problems with software.

While working with ICT in schools I noticed that people spend large amounts time 're-inventing the wheel'. Rather than ask for informa-tion or data on a disk that has already been collected, they go off and try to create their own from scratch. This is a real problem and needs a solution – but what? I think it's just a case of trying to un-teach old habits.

So much has changed since I started working at the school. One of the major technologies to affect both schools and companies is the Internet, and it has to be one of the most useful resources available. It has changed the way people communicate and work. With the birth of networked Internet in schools we have the potential to improve communications, but there are some major issues with content. I don't want to become a teacher, but I have had a chance to do some teaching. I found this to be hard and think I am better at providing support in the classroom. I do enjoy supporting lessons and think that computers are a major enhancement to the students' work – they provide a focus for those students who find it difficult. ICT can even give those students confidence in themselves and their ability, not only to produce good quality work but to help others who find technology frustrating.

My job title changed to ICT Network Manager and Support in 1998. I enjoy setting up networks and solving problems. I've set up a network at home to further my understanding of network technologies; I've found having a network useful for resolving problems and developing solutions for school.

ICT documentation

Much has been written about the documentation that schools should prepare to assist in the management of ICT (see North 1990, Tagg 1995, Donnelly 1996 and 2000, Crawford 1997, Freedman 1999). The terms policy, audit, strategy and development plan are frequently used to describe different aspects of ICT documentation, often interchangeably. Each school will have its own particular set of ICT documentation and there is no single blueprint for success. Taken together, the various items of documentation produced form an ICT handbook, the quality of which is not dependent on its size. As Freedman (1999, p. 24) has pointed out, 'it should be useful, which means accessible, not like an encyclopaedia'. When preparing ICT documentation, the question of what it should contain is best decided with another question firmly in mind – who is it for? Teachers, parents, students, Governors, advisers and inspectors are all likely to either have an interest in ICT documentation or be involved in its practical implications. However, the principal audience is the set of staff, teachers and others who implement school policies.

The ICT documentation should therefore be a guide to practice. It must be understandable and usable, but above all it should represent the ingrained working practices of the school. To be realisable, the policy guidance must take into account the current constraints inherent in the working environment. So, there is emerging a symbiotic relationship between policy and practice – policy guides practice, but practice shapes policy. An immediate result of this relationship is the need for regular updates to policy documents. This may be instigated in order to direct practice in a new direction, but equally a realisation that a better way of doing things has been discovered might lead to a change in policy. The components of ICT documentation used at Hampstead School are set out in Figure 14.

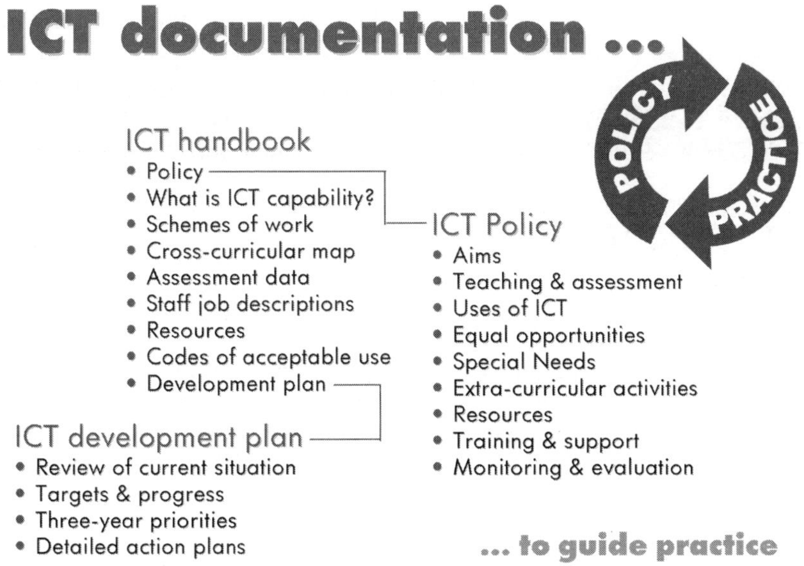

ICT documentation ...

ICT handbook
- Policy
- What is ICT capability?
- Schemes of work
- Cross-curricular map
- Assessment data
- Staff job descriptions
- Resources
- Codes of acceptable use
- Development plan

ICT development plan
- Review of current situation
- Targets & progress
- Three-year priorities
- Detailed action plans

ICT Policy
- Aims
- Teaching & assessment
- Uses of ICT
- Equal opportunities
- Special Needs
- Extra-curricular activities
- Resources
- Training & support
- Monitoring & evaluation

... to guide practice

Figure 14 Managing ICT across the curriculum – ICT documentation

The ICT Handbook contains all the basic information needed to guide practice. A simple policy has been adopted, which articulates the central aims of ICT provision and explains briefly how these aims are to be met (see Appendix 1). Some may find this too succinct, but the danger of the policy becoming an end in itself has been avoided. The ICT policy is also part of Hampstead School's Staff Guide, which contains other key policies and information. The other sections of the ICT Handbook 'flesh-out' the policy itself, by providing:

- details of how ICT capability is defined
- schemes of work setting out what is taught and assessed
- codes of practice and acceptable use (see Appendix 2)
- details of available resources
- ICT staff job descriptions.

In addition, departments are expected to include references to the use of ICT within their own departmental handbooks and schemes of work. This has helped to create 'ownership' of ICT across the school. The ICT development plan is also included in the ICT handbook, but forms a vital document in its own right. Drawing the key objectives from the whole-school improvement plan, the ICT development plan includes three-year priorities and detailed action plans for the current year. The detailed action plans set out the developmental work to be carried out during the year, the persons responsible for implementation, and the sources and amounts of funding required. The ICT development plan is updated annually (in September) in order to review the current situation and to outline progress made against targets in the previous year.

■ The funding of ICT

Funding for ICT is another major issue within schools. In order to maintain provision at the level needed to successfully implement National Curriculum requirements, meet school development objectives and adapt to rapid changes in the technology, schools need to allocate a significant budget for ICT. In addition to the main school budget, there are other potential sources of ICT funding, for which bids are often required. Every school will have its own particular set of sources for funding ICT, ranging from specialist school grants to parent-teacher association contributions. It is important to recognise that securing capital to set up a new ICT installation is just the starting point. Maintenance, replacement, furniture, software licensing, consumables, technical support, teaching staff and many other cost-carrying issues need to be taken into account. See Figure 15.

Some of the items listed represent set-up costs, while others are ongoing. However, as school ICT installations grow and develop, the distinction between these two types of spending is becoming blurred. Large secondary schools have several hundred computers, and the life-span of a PC is generally considered to be less than five years. As budgets do not normally allow mass restocking of equipment, ongoing replacement is necessary. Also, the definition of a 'consumable' item is changing – many hardware items, even monitors, now cost more to repair than to replace. These and other items that need regular replacement due to wear and tear can be considered as consumables. Software purchasing is also changing – major titles are upgraded so regularly that annual licence subscriptions make more sense than outright purchases. All of these factors mean that ICT purchases are increasingly 'ongoing' as opposed to 'one-off' in nature.

ICT expenditure

Infrastructure:
• Cabling
• Furniture
• Air conditioning

Hardware:
• Computers
• Peripherals
• Replacement

Connectivity:
• Comms hardware
• Internet services
• Connection charges

Consumables:
• Hardware items
• Print supplies
• Stationery

Software:
• New titles
• Multiple licenses
• Upgrades

Content:
• CD-ROMs
• Online material
• Web development

Staffing:
• Technical support
• Teaching staff
• Training providers

Maintenance:
• Commissioning
• Annual contracts
• Ongoing repairs

Figure 15 Managing ICT across the curriculum – funding

◼ Conclusion

There is a range of issues and challenges associated with ICT across the curriculum, for which Fullan's six 'key themes in improvement' (1991, pp. 80–8) offer a helpful management framework (as shown in Figure 16).

Vision-building is required to define and articulate the aims of the cross-curricular approach to ICT, framing them within simple policy documentation that can guide practice. Evolutionary planning allows for the adaptation of development plans as fresh needs and challenges arise. Initiative taking and empowerment result from a whole-school approach, whereby responsibility is delegated across a team. Owner-ship is extended and the vision is more likely to be shared. Monitoring and problem-solving are essential in evaluating the ICT programme, so that any obstacles to real improvement can be removed and activities redesigned. Restructuring of the timetable, staffing and resources may be necessary to create the organisational conditions conducive to a cross-curricular approach. Staff-development and resource assistance are key functions of the ICT team, and these are considered more fully in the next chapter.

Vision-building
SMT, ICT leader & ICT team
articulate aims defined
within policy documents

Evolutionary planning
Development plans are
adapted as fresh needs
& challenges arise

Restructuring
Timetabling & staffing
provide for access to ICT
resources & expertise

Initiative-taking & empowerment
Ownership & involvement
comes from delegation,
teamwork & support

Monitoring & problem coping
Evaluation of ICT
programme identifies &
deals with setbacks

Staff development & resource assistance
In-house support and team-
teaching also provides
ongoing training

Classroom & School Improvement

for improvement

Figure 16 Managing ICT across the curriculum – improvement

Main points

- Managing ICT across the curriculum is a team effort.
- An ICT leader with status is required within the school.
- The ICT team should not be set up as a traditional department – it operates in a very different way.
- Management of ICT resources has major implications for staffing and funding.
- ICT documentation should be as brief as possible to guide practice.

9 Staff development in ICT

'There is an often-expressed fear that technology will replace teachers. I can say emphatically and unequivocally, IT WON'T.'

(Gates, 1995, p. 185)

The essential role of the teacher in shaping effective ICT-based learning environments has been described earlier in the book. As new technologies have become widely used and understood in schools, so the realisation has grown that ICT supports but does not replace the teacher. The legal requirement for ICT to be used across the curriculum suggests that ICT 'needs to be every teacher's second subject' (Taylor, 1997, p. 54). However, as explained in previous chapters, it is perhaps more helpful to view ICT as a tool for learning than as an actual subject.

Increasingly, teachers are assimilating ICT into their pedagogy, developing their own ICT capability to provide opportunities for students to acquire theirs. Nevertheless, the need for further staff training in ICT is clear. Gillmon reports (1998, p. 12) that a survey carried out by the Technology Colleges Trust in 1998 concluded that 'in most schools, only a small proportion of teachers were skilled in the use of ICT'. (The 500 schools affiliated to the Trust, 47% of which are specialist schools, were asked to participate. A 55% response rate produced 10,000 completed questionnaires.)

The Government's *Survey of Information and Communications Technology in Schools 1999* (p. 23) paints a more favourable picture, stating that 'the percentage of teachers who felt confident to use ICT for teaching the curriculum was slightly higher than in 1998 and remains still around two-thirds of all teachers'. Targets for teacher development in ICT were set in *Connecting the Learning Society* (DfEE, 1997, p. 24), which states that 'by 2002 serving teachers should generally feel confident, and be competent to teach, using ICT within the curriculum'. This has led to the new TTA guidelines for ICT components of initial teacher training courses, and lottery-funded (New Opportunities Fund) ICT training for serving teachers and librarians. This chapter looks at staff development in relation to change and Hampstead School's approach, which is based on collaboration and teamwork, helping to create a 'community of practice' (Guile, 1998, p. 50).

Improvement and change

It is easy to get pulled along on the wave of change inherent in new technologies. The changeable nature of ICT is a huge strength in terms of its capacity to generate interest and excitement, but also its greatest weakness when extravagant claims are not met. There is a now-familiar process of assimilating new uses of ICT as they appear: 'over-hype by developers – adoption by enthusiasts – spread to a wider constituency of practitioners – assumption of a modest, or more significant place in the mainstream of teaching aids' (Wragg, 1997, p. 19).

There can be little doubt that ICT already occupies an increasingly 'significant place' in schools. Incorporating ICT into teaching and learning demands ongoing change, requiring careful management if it is to bring about improvement. The role of ICT as an agent of change has been recognised for some time: 'although IT is only one of a host of important factors affecting society and schools today, it is unusual among current agencies of change in that it impinges directly on the learner at all ages; on the nature and content of study; and therefore on the curriculum and the teacher' (HMI, 1989, p. 2).

The underlying purpose of staff development is to change and improve practice, which does not necessarily require specific training. As Stoll and Fink (1996, p. 164) have stated, 'many teachers and others say they do not want to "be developed" '. Instead, improvement needs to be an integral part of day-to-day practice, where 'teachers, like their pupils, must be learners' (Stoll and Fink, 1996, p. 152). Fullan (1991, pp. 37–43) has described educational change as a 'multidimensional' process, focusing on classroom practice. He identifies three key dimensions for change that relate closely to teaching and learning:

- materials;
- teaching approaches;
- beliefs.

It is easy to see how the first two dimensions would be involved in any ICT-related change. They are also clearly interrelated, as a change in teaching materials may well lead to or even necessitate new teaching approaches, and vice versa. But Fullan goes further by suggesting that effective change also requires a realignment of teachers' underlying beliefs about their practice. They need to come to terms with the reasons for change and the rationale behind any new materials or approaches. So any major change within a school would involve developments on all three dimensions. The case study that follows describes how the Internet is changing Geography teaching at Hampstead School.

■ Case study 19 – Geography

The Geography department at Hampstead School maintains its own website, which has a number of aims. It started with a collection of resources and it has developed, in an organic way, into something much more complex. There is a large collection of categorised links, which is added to all the time and students are also directed towards three or four search engines to encourage more independent research. Some of the featured sites give the students numerical and graphical challenges to test their understanding of topics such as hydrology, and they provide virtual certificates that can be printed. The department website contains collections of pictures and writing from field trips, which extends students by giving them the opportunity to publish their own work. A big chunk of the site is aimed partly at parents, containing syllabus information and recommended books, which can be ordered at Amazon.com to get a discount. Parts of the site are interactive – students can solve mystery photos and quizzes, which are fun, can consolidate learning and are an encouragement to further research. There is also a facility for students to contact staff for help with their work, which has attracted interest from students in other schools as well as Hampstead. In a new aspect of the website that we are developing, students are asked to submit a photograph showing an interest or hobby. The picture is put up on the website and then linked to Geography-related content on the Web. This helps to reinforce the fact that Geography is a real-world subject and can stimulate coursework projects that stem from the students' own interests.

The main function of the Geography website is to support what goes on in lessons, identifying and providing resources. It contains actual tasks, which can be done partly on-line and partly off-line. In one particular example, students collect some tabular population data from the website. They paste the data into a spreadsheet in order to produce graphs. The aim of the exercise is to show that the population of poor countries is often growing, while the population of richer countries is stable or declining. Students copy and paste their graphs into the word-processor and write about what they show. In the second part of the activity they visit a website that can quickly produce population pyramids of different countries. These allow students to look for more detailed population patterns. For example, in countries that have been at war the young male population is reduced; in less economically developed countries there are more older men that older women surviving, and vice versa for the richer countries. These population pyramids are copied from the website and pasted into the word-processor for analysis. In this way ICT quickly gives the students the opportunity to ask and answer the question 'Why is that?' Any aspect of ICT that gets students to ask questions is good.

Using ICT, particularly the Internet, has had many benefits for teaching and learning in Geography. It has helped to differentiate learning through the production of a range of support materials. There is still a sense of awe when using the Internet. It has a huge potential to amaze. For example, there are websites where just clicking on a button can donate several cups of food to a third-world country. Critical thinking can be encouraged by the use of on-line resources, not only through the selective use of materials. Students also have an opportunity to form critical judgements about the actions of organisations by analysing the materials that they put on the Web.

The main challenge has been acquiring the skills necessary to build a website. A one week course in webpage design during the school holidays provided a useful starting point. There is plenty of guidance available on the Web itself, but the essential ingredients have been a sense of graphical design, familiarity with graphics packages and the use of in-house expertise.

At Hampstead School, beliefs about how new technologies can improve learning opportunities have been established as a result of several years of promoting ICT as a tool for teaching, learning and administration, with strong support from senior management. The fact that ICT is treated as a cross-curricular capability, rather than as a subject in its own right, helps to shape these beliefs. For most members of staff the deployment of new resources and associated teaching approaches is welcomed because the benefits are understood. Some teachers need more persuading and it is often the supported use of ICT facilities that brings about a shift of views. So the three dimensions of 'materials', 'teaching approaches' and 'beliefs' are closely related, and one may lead to the other two.

Some teachers will use their belief in the value of ICT to try new resources and approaches, while others will develop fresh beliefs in response to new practices and facilities they have encountered. The relationship between Fullan's dimensions can be represented as a cycle of staff development and change (shown in Figure 17). 'Resources' has been substituted for 'materials' to include ICT facilities, and 'approaches' used in place of 'teaching approaches' to indicate that the cycle might apply equally to the learner as well as the teacher. The cycle may begin at any stage and can move in either direction, depending on the characteristics of the individual. A teacher may revisit each stage of the cycle many times as an initiative develops, with one change leading to another. The cycle can be 'fed into' at each of the three stages by various management interventions, examples of which are suggested. Essentially, it does not particularly matter in which order the three dimensions (or stages) are encountered by individual members of staff as there is every possibility that, with appropriate intervention, one will lead to the next. What is important is that all three are experienced for any real change to have occurred.

Figure 17 Staff development in ICT – change

The role of ICT in changing teachers' resources, approaches and beliefs has been the focus of *Apple Classrooms of Tomorrow* (ACOT) – a long-term study, begun in 1986, of the impact of new technologies in American classrooms. As the research project progressed, some major shifts were observed (Dwyer, 1994), representing change in all three dimensions. Teaching was transformed from 'didactic' and 'teacher-centred' to 'interactive' and 'learner-centred'. From a situation where the teacher was 'always expert'/'fact-teller' and the student 'always learner'/'listener', both took the part of 'collaborator' where the student was 'sometimes expert' and the teacher 'sometimes learner'. Learning was shifted away from the 'learning of facts' and 'memorisation', towards 'transformation of facts', 'relationships' and 'inquiry and invention'. The predominant use of ICT also evolved away from 'drill and practice', towards 'communication, collaboration, information access, expression', echoing the movement along the balance of control continuum described in Chapter 5.

Acquiring ICT skills

New teachers are entering the profession with ever-better ICT skills. However, many teachers with well-developed ICT skills of their own have had little experience of using ICT in the classroom with students. There are many ways in which teachers acquire ICT skills, despite the finding from the 1998 Technology Colleges Trust survey that 'the great majority of teachers had had no training in either generic or specialist applications' (Gillmon, 1998, p. 12). Many are self-taught, using skills with students in the classroom that were originally gained for other purposes. The following case study describes how one teacher at Hampstead School developed skills and confidence in ICT.

Case study 20 – Head of Year

I remember clearly the day that the first technological box landed on my desk. I was told it would make my life as Head of Year easier and it would enable me to speed up normal everyday correspondence and data-handling. This magical box would eventually transform my life. I was sceptical, a little alarmed and amused at the thought. I named him Henry. My initial challenge was how to switch it on. Of course I was shown. I was given brief instructions and told that the language used was 'basic'. Oh, how I tried those first few weeks. Every task seemed to lengthen in duration and every document I attempted seemed to disappear from the screen. Eventually defeated, I placed a poster of a skull and crossbones over the screen and left technology to those members of my team that spoke the same 'basic' language as Henry.

Haunted by guilt that I was not making use of this machine I had been given, I decided it would not beat me. My learning had begun. A notepad full of 'basic' instructions gave me the confidence to begin. With the unfailing support and encouragement of a highly competent colleague, who had vast experience in the area of special needs, I began producing letters to parents, memos to staff and minutes of meetings. I still had the skull and crossbones handy and a hard copy of everything I did. I was still not convinced but my confidence in this new technology was beginning to develop.

Computer number two arrived as I took on another responsibility for bilingual support, for which recording and analysing data was an important part. I was introduced to Excel and used it to put in figures that were needed by the school and LEA. Still feeling like a beginner, I made many errors, lost data etc. Next came my introduction to the Internet and World Wide Web. What fun I had corresponding with students who had left and gone on to university, or had gone back to their homelands. This gave me the encouragement to begin using the Web as a tool for teaching and learning. The benefits to myself, the year group and students were enormous. I have never failed to be impressed by the speed with which young people acquire ICT skills, and the sense of pride in producing a beautifully presented piece of work with spelling and grammar corrected. For my own practice I extended my teaching and learning by completing my Masters degree in PSHE. My use of ICT was extensive, not only in the writing of reports but in research that extended across the world.

In my day-to-day work I am now totally dependent on my computer. Administrative tasks take a fraction of the time. Monitoring and tracking the academic progress of 210 students has become much easier. In the area of teaching, downloading information and resources has led to my having a greater depth of knowledge. I am able to present and take educational risks that benefit my students. The greatest benefit to my students is the increased sense of pride in their achievements. A raising of their self-esteem and an ability to learn independently makes a real difference to the way in which they view school and success.

I have come along way since Henry. I now have my own PC at home and I am looking forward to learning how to install my own webpage. I have called him Ari, after Aristotle. I am very proud of him as he is 'clever' and can multi-task. I am sure that I too will be able to multi-task one day. ICT has had a great impact on my personal and professional life and this 'magical box' has certainly transformed the way in which I work. There is much learning still to be done, but enthusiasm and willingness has replaced fear and uncertainty.

Much high quality ICT training is available form LEAs, higher education establishments and other consultancies. However, a recent small-scale study, published by MirandaNet, which analyses the views of 82 teachers who regularly use or teach ICT, concludes that 'conventional ICT courses and advisory support were not able to provide all the aspects of ICT training that teachers require' (Preston, Cox and Cox, 2000, p. 3). While these forms of training can bring new ideas and approaches into the school, they rely upon a 'cascade' model of dissemination for which time must be allocated. On-site ICT training is often more immediately fruitful, as staff can develop skills using the available equipment and immediately share ideas with colleagues. School-based ICT training sessions also provide an opportunity for staff who have benefited from outside training to pass it on.

ICT teamwork as staff development

At Hampstead School, ongoing collaboration between subject teachers and ICT specialists is considered to be by far the most powerful form of staff development in ICT. External courses or expertise can lead to the introduction of new approaches, but in-house support and involvement facilitates their implementation (see also Case study 14 – Art in Chapter 6). The way in which this takes place at Hampstead School has been described in the previous two chapters, and is summarised in Figure 18.

The lottery-funded ICT training has provided an opportunity for more experienced teachers to develop their use of ICT in the classroom. This training is designed to be largely school-based and self-supported, which is a very new approach for teachers who are used to courses run by people. The human input to the lottery-funded ICT training is minimal, largely due to the cost implications. (Approximately £450 per teacher/librarian is available for the New Opportunities Fund (NOF) ICT training, which cannot be used for supply cover. Newly-qualified teachers are not eligible.) Most of the approved training providers are offering distance learning solutions, involving printed and electronic materials combined with e-mail access to ICT specialists and web-based conferencing with other participants.

The teamwork approach at Hampstead School lends itself well to these training methods, because subject teachers collaborate with in-house ICT specialists to provide a more 'human' component to the training. At the same time, the resources available through the training providers bring in additional ideas for developing and improving the

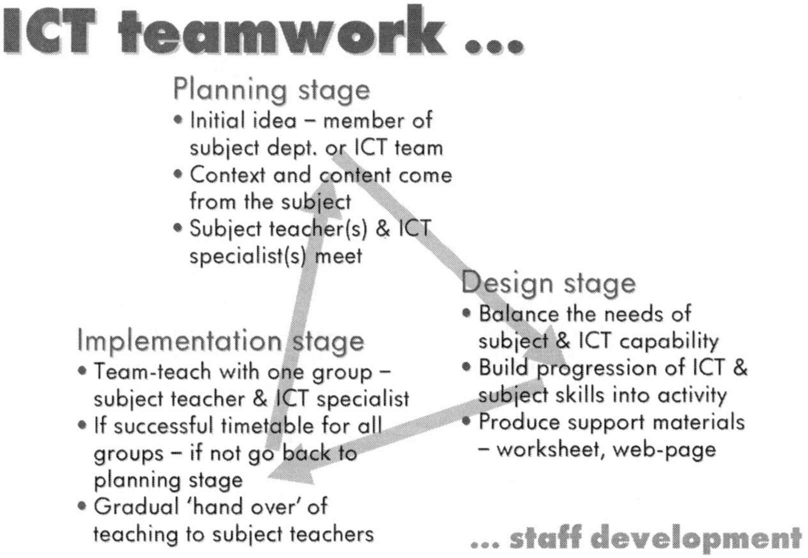

ICT teamwork ...

Planning stage
- Initial idea – member of subject dept. or ICT team
- Context and content come from the subject
- Subject teacher(s) & ICT specialist(s) meet

Implementation stage
- Team-teach with one group – subject teacher & ICT specialist
- If successful timetable for all groups – if not go back to planning stage
- Gradual 'hand over' of teaching to subject teachers

Design stage
- Balance the needs of subject & ICT capability
- Build progression of ICT & subject skills into activity
- Produce support materials – worksheet, web-page

... staff development

Figure 18 Staff development in ICT – teamwork

whole-school ICT programme. The lottery-funded training also formalises the teamwork approach, providing a framework for professional development and a means of recording each teacher's progress in integrating ICT successfully into their practice.

■ Coping with the range of software

Although ICT is an issue for all teachers, expertise across the whole range of applications is unnecessary and unreasonable to expect. At Hampstead School familiarity with *generic* applications is encouraged first and foremost, so that simple ICT-based activities can be developed that make a clear contribution to learning in the subject area taught.

There are many sound reasons for starting with generic software. Virtually every school has a basic set of generic programs, so investment in training can be built upon and applied in any teaching post. In addition to the use of ICT as a tool for learning, many teachers find generic office-type applications very useful for their own administrative tasks, such as planning, record keeping, report writing and resource production. The ICT skills acquired in learning how to use generic software are more transferable and future-proofed. The major software companies producing industry-standard generic applications spend a great deal of time and money researching the way users interact with their programs, developing friendly *user-interfaces*. They also try to ensure that many of the main features of the software are common with other programs so that when one package has been learned a significant proportion of the next can be used immediately. The introduction during the 1980s of *graphical user interfaces* (for example, Apple Macintosh and Microsoft Windows) has led to the potential for commonality across different software applications. The advent of what Gates (1995, p. 84) has called 'softer software' is the next step in making software easier to learn and use. Applications are now being programmed to adapt to the individual work patterns and needs of each user and offer 'advice' along the way. The nature of generic programs does not change enormously – they just become more sophisticated. As Cochrane (1997, p. 125) points out, 'we are moving in a direction of creating ever more complex software to perform essentially simple tasks'. Software that is more flexible and adaptable to individual needs may help to control this complexity without losing the functionality.

Specific programs, on the other hand, tend to have their own idio-syncrasies. In some cases the user-interface and tools can be non-standard in design, and valuable time is needed to master them. The content they carry may well become out-of-date or less appro-priate as time goes by. The content-free nature of generic software means it can be applied in a variety of contexts, whereas most specific programs are designed for a particular purpose. Specific software appli-cations can be added to a teacher's 'repertoire' once general confidence in ICT has been established and experience gained in using generic software with students. In the following case study a teacher describes three stages of software familiarisation as well as benefits of ICT to the teaching of English.

■ Case study 21 – English

I trained myself by getting a computer and being a user. I think it is really important to enjoy your computer and play with it. I have had some training, the best of which has been experiential – where I have taken on the role of being a student. I have focused on being able to use Microsoft Word. It is really important to have access to any programs you are going to teach with and to get to know them well. Access at home makes a real difference as well as access outside school hours. You must repeat and try things out regularly. It is vital to have a computer in the department so you can produce joint resources.

The value of teaching using ICT is that it really motivates students and significantly improves their behaviour. Students are able to learn better using ICT because it allows them to manipulate text in a way they could never do otherwise. It encourages collaborative work. It increases their linguistic awareness as they become more focused on the text. They become aware of word choice and the order of words in sentences. Students are more willing to redraft using ICT. It is particularly useful for students with learning difficulties, as they are able to produce professional work they are proud of, even though their handwriting or spelling may be very poor. It supports the development of reading skills as they get much closer to the text, are less passive and are able to interrogate the text. For example, grammar can be taught in a fun way. ICT allows students to look for different grammatical forms and see the effect of removing these. They can also reverse positives to negatives and become more aware of tone and attitude.

There are three stages to using ICT with students. At *stage one* I use different functions of Word to improve students' knowledge of language and literary techniques, for example finding a word to see how often a writer uses it. You can take Shakespeare CD-ROMs and find out how often he uses the word 'blood'! Students can manipulate text. For example, the opening of Dickens' *Bleak House* can be turned from prose into a poem, or Robert Browning's *My Last Duchess* can be turned into a script or other format. I also work with students on their own texts to help them improve their style or to become more aware of it. They can check for repetitions and use a thesaurus to add their own vocabulary. Using the outline facility allows students to look at things in terms of headings. This is particularly useful for non-fictional essay writing, as setting out the key points helps students to balance their writing at each level. Another useful exercise is taking a piece of text, such as a newspaper article, and cutting it down to size – a set number of words. This précis skill is very important. All this develops students' thinking skills.

At *stage 2* you need to purchase specialist software for students to work on spelling and accuracy – programs such as SuccessMaker. These programs require students to have a computer to themselves during the sessions for a whole term. To operate these you need to be properly trained. At *stage 3* you need the support of ICT staff to make use of other programs such as databases, spreadsheets and desktop publishing. I have used databases with English groups to create a database of books they have read plus their notes, as well as a databank of quotes they can use in their exams and coursework. I showed them how to create different fields, for genre, name, title, types of character, settings and number ratings. I have created an English area for students so they can network and learn from each other. I use desktop publishing to teach Media, incorporating articles from newspapers, to prepare the school magazine and to produce leaflets.

There have been several challenges: having enough computers can be a problem, although students also learn from having to work collaboratively together; not being able to take new programs home; students getting really frustrated when something they have prepared on one type of computer cannot be read at school; and not having enough technical support, although I have become quite good at doing things myself.

▮ Conclusion

Access to ICT facilities outside of school remains an issue. The Stephenson report (1997, p. 23) concludes that 'where teachers have access to a computer of their own, they rapidly become competent and above all confident at using it'. This is backed up by the Technology Colleges Trust survey which indicates that, although less than half of the respondents would find training using their 'own equipment' an acceptable option, teachers require 'personal access to hardware and software to facilitate regular application and development of newly acquired skills' (Gillmon, 1998, pp. 23, 25). Ownership of a computer means much more than having a grey box on the desk. A personal computer can lead to *ownership* in a much broader sense, where in some cases an anthropomorphic attitude to the machine turns it into a 'friendly assistant' (as highlighted in the Head of Year case study earlier in this chapter). This 'relationship' (often one of love and hate) helps to remove any fear, allowing teachers to take control of the technology, experiment with it, and use it for personal work and recreation as well as in their teaching. This is supported by findings from the ACOT research project: 'teachers' instructional beliefs and practices underwent an evolution, and we believed the improvement in students' competencies to be a result of teachers' personal appropriation of the technology' (Dwyer, 1994).

▇▇ Main points

■ ICT does not replace teachers, it supports and shifts their role.

■ Effective change requires a realignment of beliefs.

■ The most effective form of staff development in ICT is collaboration and support.

■ Schools need more in-house support staff for ICT.

■ Personal access leads to real ownership of ICT.

10 The 'schools' of the future

'We cannot afford poverty of vision, let alone poverty of aspiration. There are always risks in changing but the risk of failing to change is much greater.'
(Bayliss, 1999)

'We stand on the brink of a new age. Familiar certainties and old ways of doing things are disappearing. Jobs are changing and with them the skills needed for the world of tomorrow. In our hearts we know we have no choice but to prepare for this new age, in which the key to success will be the education, knowledge and skills of our people.' (Secretary of State for Education, February 1999)

The schools of the future must deliver for the future – they must deliver key skills, particularly ICT

David Hicks, speaking at the BEMAS Conference in 1998, emphasised the importance of futures thinking – cycles of envisioning, inventing, implementing, evaluating, revising and re-envisioning preferred futures. He said that no one future is now certain. We are in a world of continuous, rapid and exponential change, and this is particularly true of new technologies. We have come a long way from the one or two old BBC computers in schools to the class sets of new palm tops being brought into schools involved in the RSA project which aims to develop a new skills-based curriculum at Key Stages 3 and 4. By the time this two-year project is finished these palm tops will be well out of date.

Hicks advised all schools to help young people develop foresight, sensitivity to, and engagement with alternative futures thinking, and to reflect upon the global consequences of such changes for people and the planet. Where better to develop these than on the Internet, conferencing with students from across the world? At Hampstead we are establishing a video-conferencing link with a school in Taipei. We already have such links, mentioned earlier in the book, with schools in Spain and France. Hicks suggested the key skills needed must be imagination, creativity, analysis and logical thinking, which are all well catered for using ICT. He suggested modelling global citizenship. At Hampstead many students already play the SIMS City computer game, creating their own world civilisations.

The Report *All Our Futures – Creativity, Culture and Education* (DfEE 1999) addresses the challenges for education – creative potential, freedom and control, cultural understanding, and a systematic strategy for transforming schools to meet these challenges. 'Creative education' is defined as forms of education that develop young people's capacities for original ideas and action. 'Cultural education' is defined as forms of education that enable young people to engage positively with the growing complexity and diversity of social values and ways of life. The key recommendations include:

- A much more flexible, less content-laden curriculum and structure.

- Teachers and leaders receiving training to use methods and materials that develop young people's creative abilities and cultural understanding. This particularly requires ICT training.

- Parity of esteem between areas of experience – so delivery using ICT across the school is essential.

- Partnerships between schools, arts and cultural organisations and the communities in order to deliver creative and cultural education. ICT is the 'bait' which has the secret ingredient to 'catch' the most partners as everyone is interested and concerned to develop their own ICT skills. Schools can provide this.

- Thinking skills and dialogues encouraged in and between schools, and research into learning and the brain. ICT is superb, as we have shown in this book, at developing our thinking skills.

These recommendations can be achieved if schools use new technologies. We have already argued for an emphasis on skills and skills training. There cannot be parity of esteem if only some areas of the curriculum have access to ICT. We strongly believe that creativity within a global, culturally inclusive context is what must underpin the whole curriculum. When staff and students are given the autonomy to learn independently using ICT, and encouraged to be creative within a context of rigour and high expectations, then there will be far higher achievement.

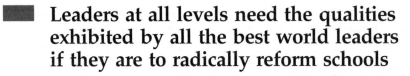

Leaders at all levels need the qualities exhibited by all the best world leaders if they are to radically reform schools

School leaders need to be committed to, and skilled in using, developing and managing ICT. They need to lead by example. Such leaders exhibit many of the characteristics picked out by Hay McBerr. The 'models of excellence' identified by Hay McBerr as the key characteristics of world-class leaders are used in the Leadership Programme for Serving Headteachers to identify five key groups of competencies needed by all school leaders. They are:

■ personal conviction, respect and value for others; the ability to both support and challenge. This means being truly and overtly convinced of the importance of ICT; respecting and valuing colleagues and being prepared to challenge the philistines amongst their staff.

■ a drive for improvement and strategic thinking. Leaders must have a powerful drive and strategies to overcome staff inertia and financial constraints. They must have the ability to overcome setbacks which are inevitable, such as Hampstead's administration triple crash.

■ social awareness and the ability to understand context. This is vital for winning over the middle of the road for parents, Governors and staff.

■ being able to make an impact and influence others. Leading means your view has to prevail on the important issues when developing ICT.

■ analytical thinking, an understanding of others and the ability to build and work in a team developing the potential of others, taking the initiative and transforming systems.

In Chapter 2 we have already stated how important it is to have clear long-term objectives:

'Schools of tomorrow must prepare students to be effective world competitors. Our task is exciting and challenging. We have to do ten things:

1. be fearless, take risks and innovate;

2. mobilise the intellectual, personal and social capabilities of all;

3. have a mission, a strategy for achieving it, ambitious goals and SMART targets by which we can monitor success;

4. *develop learning communities;*

5. *build on the strengths of all staff and students by taking their learning seriously;*

6. *support staff and students' independent learning using peer counselling, work reviews, target setting and records of achievement;*

7. *use all available information and communication technologies;*

8. *develop independent learning centres and community resources maximising new technologies which support information retrieval, information manipulation and learning;*

9. *ensure that core skills of technology, literacy and numeracy are sound;*

10. *ensure progression, credit accumulation and transfer.'*

Leading on and managing ICT will be crucial in preparing young people for uncertainties and global instabilities where all will have to continuously develop and update their skills, patterns of operation and knowledge.

The trouble with our current schools is that they were created to meet the needs of the industrial age when there were no more than 20% managerial and thinking jobs and 80% manual employment. We still have the same curriculum as in the 19th century and it is heavily content loaded at a time when there is an exponential increase in knowledge. Far more important than an overload of facts are the skills to access and select knowledge, the skills to be able to use this knowledge and to evaluate its validity, to test out theory. All of these skills are easily acquired using new technologies and taking advantage of access to a multitude of other people via the Internet.

It also used to be certain that anyone with a degree would be in employment for life. This is no longer true. First and second degrees are fast losing their currency, and a skills-based school curriculum will have far greater currency for young people seeking employment or recreation. ICT capability is a key skill vital for success, along with the broader skills of literacy and numeracy which will never lose their currency. These will raise confidence, bypass narrow cultural boundaries and actively support youngsters developing as flexible team players. We must therefore reorganise our schools to develop these skills for both teachers and students by creating active, independent learning centres where the role of the teacher is to be a lead learner and a mentor who actively supports all learners in their skills acquisition.

So how should our 'schools' be organised?

At Hampstead we have recently restructured our own School Senior Leadership Team by doing some 'futures' thinking. We arrived at three core areas of operation for the 'Learning Centre of the Future'. All three areas will be powered by and facilitated by new technologies, and each will be led by a Deputy Headteacher paired with a Senior Teacher. The three areas are:

1. support, development and outreach;
2. learning and pedagogy;
3. assessment, monitoring, evaluation and quality assurance.

We imagine that any new lead learner (teacher) or student of any age, with their family 'learning partners', will be welcomed by the 'Support, development and outreach centre' whose key objective would be to empower learners. Here, personal and social skills testimonials and portfolios, as well as appropriate activities, will be used to assess learners' confidence, their ability to understand and relate well to others, their team playing and leadership strengths, and their personal goals and action plans. Personal, peer, community and academic mentors will be assigned and they will be allocated to appropriate groups. All this work will be recorded on each student's personal data files, accessible by them as well as by staff.

The new members of this 'learning community' will move on to the 'Assessment centre' for detailed learning styles, skills, knowledge and understanding analyses and debriefing. This will rely heavily upon computer analysis and some testing but also upon the individual's skills portfolio with validated evidence of the best of his or her past experience. These portfolios, with their analyses, will be owned by the students. The students will take personal responsibility for the maintenance of their own records using technological support. Secure records will also be kept in the centre's data store in order to assist the learning centre and learner in enabling quick referral and comparative performance analysis. The key objective is to ensure that all learners are aware of their strengths and their routes for progression. So, the importance of ICT in this new kind of 'schooling' will be in the ways it facilitates everyone's awareness of both present and potential skills, knowledge and understanding.

The 'Learning centre' is the next stop for new learners, where a personal and group 'programme' will be agreed, building on existing skills and supporting further competency acquisition. Lead learners and student learners will be assigned to appropriate teams and practitioner attachments. They will be given a timetable; a programme of additional, external and independent and distance learning activities; a detailed set of learning strategies; and resources including a palmtop computer, if they do not already own one, and modem with port connections to all parts of the learning centre and other technological resources. The key objective of the learning centre is to develop multi-skilled, flexible, independent learners.

■ Teachers need to be autonomous lead learners, confident enough to actively support the development of ICT and other key skills

In this book we have made the case for all teachers to be lead learners, actively managing ICT so they transmit directly the sparkle of awareness and the competencies they have just learned (and still are close to) when they 'scaffold' other learners. This requires teachers to be given autonomy to become masters and craftspeople who will be constantly learning and seeking to improve and raise their own standards. School leaders must develop teams of teachers and students who are lifelong learning partners, who are independent, critical and unafraid to take calculated risks in respect of their reasoned and agreed agendas.

Teachers' own professional development must be taken seriously. A token five days each year is totally inadequate. Few businesses would so grossly underinvest in their workforce. All schools should work towards achieving Investors in People status where everyone has regular professional development reviews. Every school should have time for all staff to undertake serious, quality, regular professional training. Unless teachers are also learners they cannot develop new skills and ways of working. They must be able to say to their students 'do as I do'. This is exciting, and it is important that teams of learners also support each other.

Learning to use new technologies requires all of us to constantly struggle to use the latest program or machine. This challenging experience is what all learning is about! To be successful we all need support.

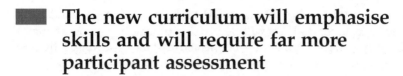

The new curriculum will emphasise skills and will require far more participant assessment

In *Redefining Schooling RSA Report* (Bayliss, 1999), the author says 'We can be sure that making schooling better does not mean more of the same.' She suggests the curriculum for the future must be the vehicle for students to demonstrate their acquisition of the vital skills, competencies and understandings. This turns the current assessment and curriculum on its head, and also makes it essential that non-school experiences must be recognised as important learning experiences.

Currently, school only occupies 15 per cent of a young person's time. Tom Bentley, Director of Demos, makes this point in his book, *Learning Beyond the Classroom* (Bentley, 1998). He says, 'Leading on and managing ICT will be crucial in preparing young people for uncertainties and global instabilities where all will have to continuously develop and update their skills, patterns of operation and knowledge.'

At Hampstead, we envisage that a new curriculum might look like the one set out below. It will be very hard, if not impossible, to manage without careful assessment and monitoring using new technologies.

Suggestions for a new curriculum

In tutorial groups

- **Relate – sessions to support getting on well and working with others:** We are just beginning to run such sessions, funded by the Excellence in Cities Initiative.

- **Philosophy, Socratic discussion:** We have carried out several pilot Socratic discussions, supported by the Society for the Furtherance of Critical Philosophy. The student evaluation has been so strongly in favour, commenting on these as being profoundly formative experiences, that we now intend to extend the pilots.

- **Citizenship modelling:** Citizenship is taught in our school as debating skills, political literacy, human rights, responsibilities, how to effect change, and being European. We also have weeks on subjects such as Refugees and the United Nations. Students must believe it is for real. Our students' councils, and the involvement of students in the selection of staff and the development of policies, make a significant difference to the students' sense of self worth, their values, respect for others and their commitment to the ethos of learning in the school. We send students to ESU debating competitions and to participate in the Model United Nations Assemblies.

■ **Thinking, logic and analysis:** There are many schools involved with the accelerated learning projects in Science and Maths (CASE and CAME), run by University College, London. The detailed evaluation shows it adds value and raises achievement across all subjects.

■ **Communications:** This needs to accentuate the spoken word and debating. Our debating societies are already making a real difference to students' awareness and their ability to articulate logical and coherent points of view. ICT, which should also be used to develop higher-order thinking skills, has vast conferencing and debating potential.

■ **Cultural heritage:** The UK has a rich cultural legacy and tradition. We are also lucky to be a truly international society. Most schools do not benefit from the richness to be drawn from Hampstead's 60% of students speaking over 80 different home languages, but both virtual and real partnerships can help make up these deficits.

■ **Creative arts:** These subjects deliver creativity and many other key skills to the whole spectrum of students in a school. They profoundly influence the environment for learning.

■ **Explorations – past, future, science, technology:** Students respond well to active participation, to stories and to discovery. Good pedagogy in these areas already takes this approach, empowering young people to develop scientific method and the concept of proof. This is significantly enhanced by new technologies.

■ **Fitness and good health:** This is vital in our unhealthy sedentary society. PE also makes a massive contribution to formative assessment and key skills.

■ **Challenges:** At Hampstead, students already take part in Duke of Edinburgh Awards, Young Enterprise schemes and ASDAN Awards. These should be integral at all levels, not just bolted on.

■ **Master classes and practitioner attachments:** At Hampstead we have seen the impact of a Head of Art commissioned to produce some artwork for television and undertaking it during lessons. The students watched in fascination and examination results shot up afterwards, as well as the teacher's 'street cred'. We should build this into the curriculum. These days we can never find staff with all the specialist skills used in business and commerce but there are many such people ready to give time and support in their area of expertise and enthusiasm.

■ **Social support / Peer tutoring:** Many schools, including ours, have success stories in this area. Using e-mail and video conferencing greatly increases the links and support that can be given.

Independent study with optional support

■ **Research, data collection and sorting**

■ **Distance learning:** Video conferencing is already happening in many schools. In ours it makes it possible both to support the gifted and talented as well as providing access to areas we cannot afford to staff. There are other benefits for the students – particularly for taking full ownership of their own learning. It also facilitates partnerships with orchestras like the London Philharmonic.

■ **Reading:** The benefits of active encouragement in the primary sector are just beginning to reach us in secondary schools, although early deprivation still holds back many.

■ **Memorisation and recall:** We need more of this and the Arts can provide valuable support.

■ **Extended writing, reports**

■ **Investigations**

Progress evaluation, target setting and recognition

■ **Portfolios** – progress evidence updates

Family learning partners – assignments and support

■ **Student management and support**
■ **Key skills acquisition and support**
■ **Research methodology**
■ **Assessment interpretation**
■ **Links with external learning partnerships**
■ **ICT at speed**

When we talk about 'family learning partners' we are recognising that for many of our students the home background may not be able to give much in the way of support. The most popular sessions we run for parents are those teaching parents skills – particularly those of ICT and understanding – to support their children's learning. This should mean that both teachers and students, together with their family learning partners 'work smarter'. That appropriate phrase was coined by John Abbott, who has made a useful distinction between that and the conventional phrase 'work harder.' That, he stresses, suited the 'Industrial Economy', but 'work smarter' is the need in today's 'Knowledge Economy' (Abbott, 1997).

The school environment is a critical factor for curriculum delivery and this is often forgotten. Even the most tatty environment can be made stimulating, a learning experience in its own right. As the Lead Judge on ICT for the 1999 Teacher Awards, Tamsyn Imison visited Moat Farm Junior School, Oldbury, outside Birmingham. This school is in an area where cars cannot be left unattended and where the school had had three lots of ICT/equipment stolen. On the last occasion, the young thieves bored through the walls to reach the computers. The only answer in the crumbling flat-roofed building was iron-barred cells. But these had been transformed into castles and palaces by young theatre designers for next to nothing. Inside the school was a grotto of delights with wonderful artefacts, activities and quality work on display. Nothing was damaged.

What we need in schools is flexible, cabled bright areas with some gentle spaces. We need meeting rooms, investigation areas, and large assembly and performance spaces. We also need decent ergonomically designed furniture, lots of original artwork and valuable, useful displays which can survive fire officers' decrees. A library and independent learning centre should be at the heart of the school. At Hampstead, we paid for ours from Technology College funding and it has already quadrupled its use. Ours is beautiful and we were inspired by the Public Library in Croydon, which everyone should visit. In the sea of concrete and gale-force winds it is a haven of beauty and a true community resource.

All this requires money. But if we are to be successful in the new global knowledge-based society we must make these investments for all our futures.

■ Key points

- The schools of the future must deliver for the future – they must deliver key skills, particularly ICT.

- Leaders at all levels need the qualities exhibited by all the best world leaders if they are to radically reform schools.

- Teachers need to be autonomous lead learners, confident enough to actively support the development of ICT and other key skills.

- The new curriculum will emphasise skills and will require far more participant assessment.

- Leading on and managing ICT will be crucial in preparing young people for uncertainties and global instabilities where all will have to continuously develop and update their skills, patterns of operation and knowledge.

Appendix 1: Hampstead School ICT Policy

Aims

1. All students have opportunities to acquire ICT Capability, as defined by the National Curriculum.
2. Staff and students are able to use ICT to enhance learning across the curriculum.
3. Staff and students can easily access ICT resources and their ICT work.
4. Students are encouraged to become independent users of ICT, and ICT is used to promote independent learning.
5. Training, support and encouragement are available from the ICT Team when needed.

Teaching of ICT Capability

The school has a cross-curricular approach to the teaching of ICT Capability. Students use ICT resources within their subjects to acquire ICT Capability and to enhance learning. The programme of ICT activities across the curriculum provides an ICT entitlement for all students:

- Most departments provide ICT activities at all stages, which are integrated into schemes of work.
- ICT activities are designed by ICT staff working with the department concerned.
- ICT activities are designed to enhance learning within the subject.
- ICT activities are designed to teach particular aspects of ICT Capability.
- As far as possible ICT activities are timetabled in advance so that resources and support are available.

- Assessment criteria (NC levels) for ICT Capability are built into each activity.

- During Year 9, ICT work is assessed formally to determine a level of ICT Capability for each student.

- ICT activities are regularly reviewed and updated by subject staff and the ICT Team.

In addition to the entitlement programme, ICT is used to support and enhance teaching and learning in an ongoing way, and students are encouraged to use ICT independently to develop and improve their work.

Assessment of ICT Capability

During Year 9, the portfolio of ICT work that students have built up is assessed formally and a National Curriculum level is awarded and reported to students and parents. The levels of ICT Capability within the National Curriculum Attainment Target for Information & Communication Technology only apply at Key Stage 3.

At Key Stage 4 and Post-16, students can use the National Inter-Action Computing Award Scheme (NICAS) to gain certificates in major ICT applications, including word processing, databases, spreadsheets and desktop publishing. From September 2000, all Key Stage 4 and Post-16 students will be entered for the ICT Key Skills award. A new advanced GNVQ in ICT is being offered to Post-16 students from September 2000.

Other Uses of ICT

There are other uses of ICT that do not necessarily contribute to the acquisition of ICT Capability, but can enhance learning. These come under the general heading computer-assisted learning (CAL) and include:

- Practice and revision programs, and educational games – to introduce or reinforce concepts, facilitate group work or role-play and promote independent learning.

- Integrated Learning Systems (ILS) – to teach, reinforce and assess parts of the curriculum for students working independently. *SuccessMaker* is used by all Year 7 students for numeracy and literacy support.

▰ The Internet

The Internet World Wide Web is available to staff and students across the network for use in both lessons and extra-curricular activities. Internal and external filtering is used to help prevent student access to unsuitable material. All staff are allocated a personal e-mail address and students can apply for one – applications require parental approval. Students are expected to follow the school's Internet Code when using the Internet. The school's website (HYPERLINK http://www.hampsteadschool.org.uk www.hampsteadschool.org.uk) is used to provide key information for students, parents and the wider community. The website is currently being developed to include a wider range of general information and also more subject-based resources to support learning.

▰ Extra-Curricular Activities

In addition to planned ICT activities, students have access to the ICT facilities for improving and enhancing their work. These opportunities allow further acquisition and consolidation of ICT Capability and enable students to work and learn independently. The ICT facilities in the Independent Learning Centre (ILC) are available for students at break, lunchtime and after school most days. Priority is given to students who want to continue with their school work. Sixth form students have access to their own ICT facilities on the mezzanine floor of the ILC at all times of the day. Other subject-specific, extra-curricular ICT activities are provided within department areas.

▰ Equal Opportunities

Equality of opportunity for all students is central to the provision of ICT across the curriculum at Hampstead School and the ICT Team follows the whole school Equal Opportunities policy. The principle of entitlement underlies the programme of ICT Activities and the open access to resources outside of lessons.

▰ Special Educational Needs

It is recognised that ICT has much to offer in supporting students with special needs, and the ICT team follows the school's Special Needs

Policy. Students are supported by the provision of suitable ICT resources and software; step-by-step instruction sheets; one-to-one support where necessary; extension activities for experienced students.

ICT Support and Training

Whenever possible, ICT staff will be present to teach ICT Capability, support subject learning and provide technical support when ICT is being used. The ICT staff are available to support departmental uses of ICT, using both centralised and departmental resources, by team teaching, production of ICT support materials and INSET sessions. The ICT team offers staff INSET sessions on general ICT applications. In addition, departmental ICT INSET is offered for training in subject-specific ICT skills and for developing ICT activities. Individual ICT training can also be arranged. Details of courses offered by higher education establishments and other training agencies are disseminated. Staff can also use NICAS to gain accreditation for their ICT skills. Staff are encouraged and supported in taking advantage of ICT training funded through the New Opportunities Fund.

Management of ICT Resources

ICT resources are as integrated as possible, to allow staff and students easy access to their work wherever they are in the school. This is facilitated by networking computers within the various parts of the school. Staff and students have individual user areas on the school's RM Network. Central ICT resources are managed by ICT staff for use by all. ICT rooms are timetabled in advance for some ICT activities and can be booked at other times. Many departments have their own ICT resources, again managed by the ICT team. The Director of ICT works with staff to identify future resources requirements to meet the needs of the school.

Health and Safety

The ICT Team follows the school's Health and Safety Policy. In addition, the ICT Safety & Security Code and the ICT Internet Code are displayed in all areas containing ICT resources. There is a long-term aim to improve the ergonomics of some of the workstations around the school.

New Technologies and Techniques

The ICT Team will keep up with and advise on new technologies and new approaches to teaching and learning with ICT. A range of ICT journals, magazines and catalogues is available for staff to browse and borrow.

 # Monitoring & Evaluation

Implementation of the ICT Policy is monitored in an ongoing way, through regular meetings of members of the ICT Team and of the team as a whole, and through meetings with Heads of Department and other staff. The key questions for evaluating the effectiveness of ICT provision are based on the aims of this policy:

- Does the use of ICT support the acquisition of ICT Capability?

- Does the use of ICT lead to the enhancement of subject teaching?

- Do ICT systems function adequately and reliably?

- Can staff and students access and use ICT facilities easily and effectively?

- Are staff and students adequately supported in their use of ICT?

In addition, monitoring takes place annually as part of the ICT development plan, including a review of the current situation and progress against targets set.

Appendix 2: Hampstead School ICT Codes

Information & Communications Technology

Safety & Security Code

<u>Please</u> follow the points below when using ICT facilities.

1 **Always treat ICT equipment with care:**
 • if ICT equipment is faulty, tell a member of staff;
 • do not try to fix things yourself;
 • do not tamper with cables or connections.

2 **Adjust ICT equipment for maximum comfort:**
 • keyboards, mice and monitors can be adjusted;
 • do not try to move the base unit – damage can be caused;
 • leave ICT equipment tidy when you have finished.

3 **Do not take food or drink near computers:**
 • food can stick to the keyboard or mouse, causing problems;
 • liquid can cause serious damage.

4 **Look after your user account:**
 • choose a password that is easy to remember and that nobody else will guess;
 • do not tell anyone else your password;
 • if you forget your password, see a member of ICT staff;
 • you **must not** try to use anyone else's user account.

5 **Use your network user space properly:**
 • your network user space is for storing your work files;
 • you **must not** save files that are racist; sexist, obscene or offensive to others;
 • you **must not** copy computer programs into your user space;
 • you **must not** try to tamper with anyone else's user space.

6 **Use printers properly:**
 • printers are for printing your school work;
 • you **must not** print multiple copies of your work;
 • you **must not** print anything other than school work.

Your use of ICT facilities will be monitored by members of staff.

Information & Communications Technology

Internet Code

Please follow the points below when using the Internet.

1 The **World Wide Web** (WWW) is available to help you with your work. You may also look up information that interests you, but students wishing to do their school work have priority access.

2 Students are expected to be responsible when accessing information on the WWW. You **must not** attempt to access information that is racist, sexist, obscene or offensive to others.

3 Information on the WWW varies in quality. It can be very useful, but not all of it is reliable. Always identify the source of the information and check that it is relevant.

4 When you use information from the WWW in your own work:
• do not pretend it's your own;
• write down the source (say where it came from);
• compare it with other available information;
• add your own ideas and views.

5 **Electronic mail** (e-mail) is available for you to make contacts with others who might help you with your work.

6 Students are expected to be responsible when using e-mail. You **must not** use e-mail in any way that could be harmful or distressing to others.

7 Do not waste time sending e-mail to people who you can just as easily speak to.

8 When communicating with others using e-mail:
• always use appropriate language;
• do not give your personal details to strangers;
• never arrange to meet strangers;
• do not respond to bad messages.

Your use of the Internet will be monitored by members of staff. Students failing to follow this code will have their Internet access removed.

Appendix 3: Hampstead School Cross-curricular ICT Map (1999–2000)

	Year 7	Year 8	Year 9	Years 10 & 11
English	Word processing of poems, incorporating graphics where appropriate.	Writing a book review and incorporating a scanned book cover (possibly re-designed).	Producing a poster and other promotional material for an advertising campaign incorporating text and graphics (Kif drinks).	Coursework – drafting and presentation.
Maths	Data handling activity – collecting data about themselves, entering it into a database, analysing data by searching sorting, graphing, etc. LOGO activities – drawing shapes, investigating patterns. Spreadsheet modelling – planning a party. Geometry modelling using Geomat – rotation & reflection. Use of Internet for research, e.g. famous mathematicians, counting systems	Spreadsheet modelling – exploring formulas. LOGO activities – drawing shapes, investigating polygons. Data handling activity – analysing and presenting data about how students travel to school by searching, sorting, graphing, etc. Using Omnigraph to create linear graphs and explore equations. Use of Internet for research, e.g. famous mathematicians, counting systems.	LOGO activities – developing instructions to generate and transform shapes and paths. Spreadsheet modelling of straight line graphs. Headstart – introduction for Higher and Intermediate groups. SuccessMaker – for foundation groups.	Graphing and function-plotting activities using Omnigraph, including: linear, quadratic and cubic equations, and transformations of graphs.

Science	Data-logging activities, particularly 'Hot Potatoes' – collecting and presenting data from simple experiments using temperature probes.	Data-logging activities – collecting and presenting data from experiments using temperature probes. Modelling electrical circuits using Crocodile Clips, then creating some of the circuits with real apparatus.	Data-logging activities – collecting and presenting data from experiments using a range of probes. Modelling activity – using and evaluating the Creatures simulation. Data retrieval and analysis – using Internet/Intranet, CD-ROMs.	Research for and presentation of coursework. Data-logging activities – collecting and presenting data from experiments using a range of probes. Modelling electrical circuits using Crocodile Clips.
Design & Technology	Control – designing a traffic light system (project lasting half a term).	Graphic design – creating a chocolate bar wrapper using graphics programs. Control – controlling a sliding door model (project lasting half a term).	Villa project: producing and plotting a floorplan using a CAD program, using a spreadsheet to model costings.	Research for and presentation of coursework, including graphics, wordprocessing, DTP, CD-ROMs, Internet: • Music promotional project • Free gift project • Graphic design business paper and card.
History	Was King John an evil king? – simple word-processing activity and creating a gravestone with epitaph for King John using a graphics program. The Black Death/ Peasants Revolt – creating a newspaper page. Cut and paste word-processing activity examining Martin Luther's role in the Reformation.	Causes of the English Civil War – cut and paste word-processing activity and writing frame. Creating graphs to show population increases during Industrial Revolution, incorporating graphs into a report. Creating spreadsheet to analyse reasons for Charles I lack	Creating a news-paper article about Little Rock or Montgomery Bus Boycott, incorporating various sources including graphics. Producing graphs on WW1 Causes using spreadsheet. Incorporating graphs into report for cabinet ministers. WW2 Propaganda – manipulating photos, producing newspaper article.	Germany in the Depression – designing a spreadsheet and producing graphs in Excel. Research for and presentation of coursework.

History	Creating Mughal Indian tiles with a graphics program. Why Did Towns Grow in the Renaissance? – wordprocessing activity, creating a table.	of popularity, pasting this as popularity, pasting as a table in a WP to answer questions Database analysis of living/ working conditions in the Industrial Revolution, with written report.		
Geography	'Safe routes to school' activity using MapMaker. Introductory Internet exploration activities.	Regeneration of Kilburn activity using MapMaker. Using Excel to produce population graphs for interpretation in the wordprocessor. Internet exploration activities.	Using the Internet to research the Kobe Earthquake, then using a word-processor to present a report.	Research for and presentation of coursework.
Modern Languages	Creating an identity card in French/Spanish. Setting up and interrogating a birthdays database and/or designing a birthday card. Designing a café or restaurant menu. Creating a time-table in French/Spanish.	Producing a weather forecast based on a weather map. Producing a cartoon character and writing a description in French or Spanish.	Designing and producing a leaflet in French advertising a club, incorporating graphics. Making posters in Spanish of favourite films and musicians. Tengo hambre – sorting activity and designing a restaurant menu.	Research for and presentation of coursework. Designing a leaflet about London for a French/Spanish speaking visitor.
Art	Simple animation, creating frames and sequencing them. Simple manipulation and modelling of digital images.	Manipulation and modelling of digital images.	More advanced manipulation and modelling of digital images.	Digital image capture, manipulation and modelling.

Music	History of the orchestra – researching different types of orchestra then designing an information sheet/webpage.	Popular music – researching different types of popular music then designing an information sheet/webpage. Using sequencing software to build on a simple chord pattern, using drums, basslines and melodies.	Using sequencing software for composition and presentation.
Drama			Researching and presenting coursework.
PE	Wordprocessing self-assessments.	Wordprocessing self-assessments.	Wordprocessing self-assessments. Data-logging of pulse rates before and after exercise.	Using CD-ROMs and the Internet to research GCSE topics (including physiology).
Careers			Interrogation of careers databases – Kudos, KeyClips, CareerScape.	Wordprocessing of NRA student statements.

References and bibliography

Abbott, J. (1997) 'Speech to the Council of Scientific Societies, Washington', *CSSP Journal*.

Bayliss, V. (1998) *Redefining Schooling*, RSA.

Bentley, T. (1998) *Learning Beyond the Classroom*, Demos and Routledge.

Binney, G. and Williams, C. (1995) *Learning into the Future*, Nicholas Brearly.

Birnbaum, I. (1990) *IT in the National Curriculum: Some Fundamental Issues*, Resource.

Brown, J. and Howlett, F. (1994) *IT Works: Stimulate to Educate*, BECTA (formerly NCET).

Bruner, J. (1996) *The Culture of Education*, Harvard University Press.

Cochrane, P. (1997) *Tips for Time Travellers*, Orion Business Books.

Cook, D. and Finlayson, H. (1999) *Interactive Children, Communicative Teaching*, Open University Press.

Cox, M. J. (1997) *The Effects of Information Technology on Students' Motivation*, NCET.

Crawford, R. (1997) *Managing Information Technology in Secondary Schools*, Routledge.

Dennison, B. and Kirk, R. (1990) *Do – Review – Learn – Apply: a simple guide to experiential learning*, Blackwell.

Dewey, J. (1916) *Democracy and Education*, Macmillan.

DFE (1995) *Information Technology in the National Curriculum*, HMSO.

DfEE (1997) *Connecting the Learning Society*, DfEE.

DfEE (1999) *Creativity, Culture and Education*, DfEE.

DfEE/QCA (1999) *Information and Communication Technology – The National Curriculum for England*, DfEE/QCA.

Donnelly, J. (1996) *IT and Schools*, Croner.

Donnelly, J. (2000) *ICT and the Learning Revolution*, SHA.

Dwyer, D. (1994) 'Apple classrooms of tomorrow: what we've learned' in *Educational Leadership*, 51(7): 4–10.

Freedman, T. (1999) *Managing ICT*, Hodder & Stoughton.

Fullan, M. (1991) *The New Meaning of Educational Change*, Cassell.

Fullan, M. (1995) *International Handbook of Educational Leadership – Leadership for Change*, Kluwer.

Gardner, H. (1993) *Multiple Intelligences: the Theory in Practice*, Basic Books.

Gates, B. (1995) *The Road Ahead*, Viking.

Gillmon, E. (1998) *Building Teachers' ICT Skills: The Problem, and a Framework for the Solution*, TC Trust.

Goleman, D. (1995) *Emotional Intelligence – Why it can Matter More than IQ*, Bloomsbury.

Guile, D. (1998) *Information and Communication Technology and Education*, Institute of Education, University of London.

Healy, J. M. (1999) *Failure to Connect: How Computers Affect Our Children's Minds – and What We Can Do About It*, Touchstone.

HMI (1989) *Curriculum Matters 15: Information Technology From 5 to 16*, HMSO.

Honey, P. and Mumford, A. (1992) *The Manual of Learning Styles*, Peter Honey.

Kolb, D. A. (1984) *Experiential Learning: Experience as the Source of Learning and Development*, Prentice Hall.

Lockitt, B. (1997) *Learning Styles: Into the Future*, FEDA.

McKinsey and Co (1997) *The Future of Information Technology in Schools*, McKinsey and Co.

NACCE (1999) *All our Futures*: DfEE.

National Curriculum Council (1990), *Non-statutory Guidance – Information Technology Capability*, NCC.

North, R. (1990) *Managing Information Technology: The Role of the IT Coordinator*, University of Ulster.

OFSTED (2000) *The Annual Report of Her Majesty's Chief Inspector of Schools – Standards and Quality in Education 1998/99*, The Stationery Office.

OFSTED (2000) *Hampstead School OFSTED Short Report*, The Stationery Office.

Pachler, N. (1999) 'Theories of Learning and ICT', Leask, M. and Pachler, N. (eds.), *Learning to Teach Using ICT in the Secondary School*, Routledge.

Papert, S. (1980) *Mindstorms: Children, Computers and Powerful Ideas*, Harvester Wheatsheaf.

Preston, C., Cox, M. and Cox, K. (2000) *Teachers As Innovators – An Evaluation of the Motivation of Teachers to Use Information and Communications Technologies (Full Summary)*, MirandaNet.

Russell, B. (1926) *On Education*, George Allen & Unwin Ltd.

Sammons et al (1995) *Key Characteristics of Effective Schools*: Institute of Education.

SCAA (1995) *Key Stage 3 – Information Technology, the New Requirements,* SCAA.

SCAA (1995) *Key Stage 3 – Information Technology and the National Curriculum,* SCAA.

SCET (1996) *Information Ethics: A Guide for Managers in Scottish Schools,* SCET.

Schofield, J. W. (1995) *Computers and Classroom Culture,* Cambridge University Press.

Smart, L. (1996) *Using IT in Primary School History,* Cassell.

Statistical Bulletin (1999), *Statistics of Education – Survey of Information and Communications Technology in Schools 1999,* The Stationery Office.

Stenhouse, L. (1980) *Curriculum Research and Development in Action,* Heinemann.

Stephenson, D. (1997) *Information and Communications Technology in UK Schools – An Independent Inquiry,* The Independent ICT in Schools Commission.

Stoll, L. and Fink, D. (1996) *Changing Our Schools: Linking School Effectiveness and School Improvement,* Open University Press.

Tagg, B. (1995) *Developing a Whole School IT Policy,* Pitman.

Taylor, P. (1997) 'IT: Every Teacher's Second Subject', Heilbronn, R. & Jones, C. (eds.) *New Teachers in an Urban Comprehensive School,* Trentham.

Tharp, R. G. and Gallimore, R. (1991) 'A Theory of Teaching as Assisted Performance', in Light P. (ed), *Learning to Think,* Routledge.

Watkins, C. et al (1998) *Learning About Learning,* NAPCE.

Watkins, C. (2000) 'Feedback between teachers', Askew, S. (ed.), *Feedback for Learning,* Routledge.

Wood, D. (1988) *How Children Think and Learn*: Blackwell.

Wood, D. (1998) *The UK ILS Evaluations – Final Report,* BECTA/DfEE.

Wragg, E. C. (1997) *The Cubic Curriculum,* Routledge.

Index

access 57–8, 137
active experimentation 53
aims and objectives 135–6
Art curriculum 77–8
assessment 39, 40–41, 136
    archives 41–2

balance of control 70–71

CAD/CAM 64, 94
co-ordinators, ICT 100
codes, ICT 58, 137, 140–41
communications, internal 35,
    101
computers, learning tools 48–9
confidentiality 27–8
crashes 24, 26–7
cross-curricular approach
    curriculum 142–5
    ethos 20–21, 86
    ICT in 84–6, 114, 125
    logistics 87
    organisation 87
cultural education 125
curriculum development 38–9,
    127, 130–32
    see also subjects by title

data
    protection 26, 27–8
    student 35
data-logging 67–8, 91, 94, 100–1
Design and Technology (D&T)
    curriculum 63–4, 93–4, 96

do-review-learn-apply learning
    cycle 54–6
documentation, ICT 106–8

e-mail clubs 92, 93
educational enhancement 88–9, 90,
    99
English curriculum 91, 121–2
enthusiasm, students 48–9
equal opportunities 137
ethical policies 19–20
examination courses, ICT 94–5
examinations, administration
    29–31
executive, role of 100

finance, budgeting 32

GCSE 41
Geography curriculum 91,
    113–14
governors, role of 13–14, 100

Hampstead School 2–5
hardware, upgrading 25
Headstart 69
health and safety 25–6, 138
History curriculum 91, 100–1

independent study 132
information overload 24–5
integrated learning systems (ILS)
    68
integration, ICT 84, 85–6

inter-departmental co-operation
38, 68, 87
Internet
access 58
codes 58, 137, 140–41
uses 105–6, 114, 124, 137

leadership 11, 126–7, 129
learning centres, independent 21,
57–8, 128–9
learning environments 63, 67,
71–2
learning processes 49–50, 53
do-review-learn-apply cycle
54–6
higher level 56
types 65–6
LOGO 69–70

management
attendance 35–6
efficiency 26
ICT 99–100, 101, 106–8
integration 22–3, 100, 101
Maths curriculum 68–70, 91, 94
Media Studies curriculum 96–7
Modern Languages curriculum 91,
92–3
monitoring and evaluation 42–7,
102–3, 109–10, 139
Music 2000 80–81
Music curriculum 80–82, 91

National Curriculum 2000 74,
75–6, 85
Nova T 36–7

parents
communication with 23
learning partners 132–3
partnership schools 93
PE curriculum 94
presentation, student work 39
printing services 57
problem solving 50–52
process orientation 76

progression 78–80, 82, 121–2
publishing 28–9

record keeping 22
research, student 54, 113
resources
economy of 52
funding 108–9
management 103–5, 138
replacement 108–9

school improvement plans 23,
37–9, 101, 108, 126–7
monitoring and evaluation 42–7,
102–3
schools, future 10, 124–34
Schools Information Management
System (SIMS) 27–8
Assessment Manager 40–41
Science curriculum 50–53, 66–8, 94
Secondary Heads Association
(SHA), IT policy 14–19
security 26
software
Cash Accounts 32
choice 36
generic 61–2, 63–4, 66, 119–20
licences 109
specific 61–2, 66, 120
student training 64
special educational needs 21, 121,
137–8
staff development 111–12, 112–13,
115–16, 129, 138
distance learning 118–19
funding 12, 118
staffing structure 101
status, ICT 73–4, 99, 112
students
assessment 39, 40–42
attendance 35–6
data 35
enthusiasm 48–9
pre-skills 64
SuccessMaker 68–9
support, external 23

teacher–student partnerships 129
teachers
 computer ownership 122–3
 cover administration 36–7
 initial training 111, 116
 learning process 23, 116–18
 personal development 116–18
 roles 49–50, 60–61, 111

teaching, supportive 49
technical support 103–5, 105–6
timetabling 34

video-conferencing 125

websites, school 113–14